JESUS CHRIST THE ONLY WAY

JESUS CHRIST
THE ONLY WAY

Christian Responsibility in a
Multicultural Society

edited by

Patrick Sookhdeo

EXETER
THE PATERNOSTER PRESS

AUSTRALIA
Emu Book Agencies Pty., Ltd.,
63, Berry Street, Granville,
N.S.W. 2142

SOUTH AFRICA
Oxford University Press,
P.O. Box 1141, Buitencingle Street,
Cape Town

British Library Cataloguing in Publication Data

Jesus Christ the only way.
   1. Christianity – Great Britain
   2. Christianity and other religions
  I. Sookhdeo, Patrick
  261.2   BR759

ISBN 0–85364–236–2

Printed in Great Britain by
Redwood Burn Limited
Trowbridge & Esher

Contents

Part Three: They Speak for Themselves

Preface

ON APRIL 10, 1975, THE ASSEMBLY OF THE EVANGELICAL alliance, meeting at Bristol, passed the following resolution: 'This Assembly, conscious of the growing presence of non-Christian faiths in Britain and of the increase in opportunities for Christian witness, urges the Evangelical Alliance to set up a commission to study both theologically and practically a Christian approach to those of other faiths. ... The aim of the Commission should be in the current atmosphere of religious syncretism to clarify the issues of inter-faith dialogue and to help local churches present the gospel unequivocally and yet with understanding to those of other cultures and beliefs.'

Jesus Christ the Only Way is the response to this resolution. It is based upon meetings of the Commission and upon a number of documents, some of which were written by members specifically for this purpose. Chapters 4 and 5, in particular, include some insights and material from papers written by Dr. Kwame Bediako, Mr. H. L. Ellison, Dr. Myrtle Langley, Dr. Eric Sharpe, Rev. Hugh Silvester, Mr. Patrick Sookhdeo, Rev. A. C. Thiselton, and Mr. W. Walker.

The section, 'They speak for Themselves' is contributed by well-known adherents of non-Christian faiths. These chapters are not primarily intended to provide information about the beliefs and practices of these faiths although some chapters contain a good deal of such information. They are important especially because they show what the authors think it most important to tell British Christians about the religious communities they represent. As such, these final chapters claim serious attention.

A selection of extended essays relating to inter-faith dialogue and resulting from the work of the Commission is due for publication during 1979.

Part One

Setting the Scene

1

The Impact and Influence of non-Christian Religions

GILBERT KIRBY

ANYONE CONCERNED FOR THE WELL-BEING OF THE COMMUNITY as a whole must be alarmed by the efforts being made in certain quarters in Britain today to foment race hatred. Our concern here, however, is not so much with the problem of race as such but rather with the fact that in many cases those of other races also represent other religions and that these non-Christian religions are becoming firmly established in a country which hitherto has at least paid lip service to the over-riding claims of the Christian faith. Before we proceed further, and in order to prevent misunderstanding later on, it might be as well if we defined our terms.

Our concern is with the impact of other faiths on Britain today. It is true, of course, that the vast majority of those who adhere to these non-Christian religions are those who have come to these shores from overseas. The word 'immigrant' is somewhat loosely used to describe such people, although many of them are, in fact, British citizens with British passports to prove the point!

By no means all 'immigrants' are 'coloured' people and not all of them represent 'other faiths'. We have Christians drawn from many different racial and cultural backgrounds who have come as immigrants into Britain – some from Africa, some from Asia, some from Latin America and yet others from the continent of Europe and from Eire. We now have thousands of men and women in Britain who represent what are termed the ethnic religions of the world – religions which are usually associated with a particular race. Even so, we shall find there are, for example, Englishmen who have embraced the Bud-

11

dhist faith, or have become Muslims, just as there are Muslims who have become Christians. We are not, therefore, primarily concerned with race or colour but with creed. It does so happen that most Muslims in Britain are dark-skinned and almost all Hindus come from India and East Africa, but we are anxious to know what impact their presence in Britain is having. As recently as 1950 there were approximately 100,000 'coloured people' living in Britain. Not all of these, of course, would necessarily be adherents of non-Christian religions. From about 1948 there was a steady trickle of West Indians coming into Britain in search of employment, and the vast majority of these had Christian backgrounds. From 1954 onwards Commonwealth citizens came into the United Kingdom in larger numbers, so that between 1955 and 1957 the immigrant population doubled, and, of course, since then there has been a further increase. The door was kept fairly wide open until the Commonwealth Immigration Act of 1962 and subsequent Acts restricted entry. Politicians of the right and the left have debated the question of limiting the number of immigrants on various grounds. Meanwhile ordinary people with different ethnic, cultural and religious backgrounds are slowly learning to live and work in harmony. It is estimated that there are about 2,000,000 people from racial minority groups living in Britain, almost half of whom are in the Greater London area.

Asian Religions

Islam is the second largest religious group in Britain. There are probably between 600,000 and one million Muslims in the United Kingdom. In 1976 the 'World of Islam Festival' created a good deal of interest in Islam and two years later the new Central Mosque in Regent's Park was opened. In 1945 there was one mosque in the whole of England, today there are at least 200. We do not always take sufficiently into account that one in every seven people in the world is a Muslim. Christianity has made little headway in such predominantly Muslim lands as those of North Africa and Muslims themselves tend to regard Christianity as a declining force.

The largest proportion of Muslims in the United Kingdom

comes from Pakistan. In places such as Bradford and Peterborough Pakistanis represent the largest immigrant group. To the average Pakistani, Britain is a foreign land, whose language, customs, religion, and way of life are almost totally alien to what he has known. It must be remembered that Pakistan is an Islamic state which owes its existence and separate identity to the practice of Islam. For Pakistanis, therefore, Islam is an expression of patriotism as well as a religion.

Most Pakistanis in Britain are of rural origin and not surprisingly find adjustment to western society difficult. They tend to live in their own closely-knit communities, largely served by their own shops and other facilities provided by their countrymen. They, on the whole, retain links with the land of their birth and many cling to the so-called myth of return.

Pakistanis are very much bound together by family ties and the head of the family exercises very real authority. Of course, not all the Muslims in Britain today come from Pakistan. There are sizeable Arab, Bengali, Turkish and African Muslim communities.

The overwhelming majority of immigrants from India are either Hindus or Sikhs. The latter have received considerable press publicity because many of the men insist upon wearing turbans which to them is a requirement of their religion. Sikhs tend to be houseproud and set out to purchase their own properties. They naturally like to remain alongside their friends and near to the gurdwara (Sikh temple). They are probably the most homogenous, the most cohesive and best organised of any immigrant group. Theirs is a cohesion of people who throughout their existence have been a minority fighting for survival. As a group they have a long migratory tradition in many parts of the world. The strongest religious, cultural and social focus of the Sikh community in any town where Sikhs have settled is the gurdwara. The president of the gurdwara is the titular head of the community. Most of the Sikhs in Britain come from the Punjab region of India. One of the facilities provided by the gurdwara is the provision of classes for children. The custom of arranged marriages is still widely accepted by young Sikhs.

The estimated number of Hindus in Britain is 250,000.

13

Most of these are located in and around London, in the Midlands and in Liverpool, Leeds and Newcastle. In Leicester there are some 25,000 Hindus and in Birmingham 10,000. Generally speaking, the British public is less well informed about Hindu beliefs and practices than about Islam. This is partly because Hinduism itself is so complex and so far removed from traditional western thought-patterns. On the whole Hindus in Britain will probably still in some way celebrate the annual festival of Divali (a festival of lights, but also of the victory of good over evil, and of family loyalties). There are also Jains and Parsis in Britain today, but their numbers are relatively small.

Anyone at all familiar with areas where there are many concentrations of Asians will have detected certain racial characteristics. Many Asians in a given community tend to come from the same area in the land of their birth. Thus, almost all the Bengali community in East London hails from the Sylhet region in Bangladesh, and a very large percentage of Pakistanis in Peterborough is drawn from the district of Mirpur, which was formerly part of the state of Jammu and Kashmir. Many have considerable difficulty in speaking English, particularly the women. Family ties are both stronger and more extended than with the average Britisher. In most Asian families the authority of the oldest male member still counts for a great deal. He has authority over all others even when they are married, and he is responsible for their needs being met. Asians are much less individualistic in outlook than most westerners. The older Asians regard with considerable alarm the permissiveness which characterizes Britain today. Asian religion affects every aspect of life and is often a rebuke to the nominalism of all too many professing Christians.

Mysticism

We have not referred as yet to the Buddhist community. Buddhism has had an appeal especially to certain intellectuals probably the most notable of whom is Christmas Humphreys Q.C. In November 1974 the Buddhist Society, with headquarters in Eccleston Square, London, completed its first fifty years of work in Britain. As a religious philosophy Buddhism represents a wide variety of doctrine and practice. It has special appeal in an age of syncretism. It has been described as 'the philosophy of nothingness'. God in the objective personal sense does not fit into the system. Buddhists adhere to the twin doctrine of Karma and rebirth.

Undoubtedly, one of the religious side effects of the presence of Buddhists and Hindus in Britain has been to arouse intensive interest in eastern mysticism. As R. D. Clements points out in his booklet, *God and the Gurus* (Inter Varsity Press), 'Dancing figures chant the names of gods in Oxford Street; guileless, tranquil gurus smile beneficently down from the advertising hoardings on scurrying, busy London office-workers; the East has come West. Christians, whose major foe in recent times has been materialism, have suddenly to confront an alternative philosophy which is quite blatantly spiritual in emphasis.

The three best known Eastern sects in Britain are the Divine Light Mission, the International Society for Krishna Consciousness and Transcendental Meditation. The Divine Light Mission is a Vedantist Hindu movement based on devotion to the Guru, Maharaj Ji, who claims to give enlightenment to his disciples. The Guru claims: 'In this age of darkness I have come to reveal light.' The Divine Light Mission uses meditative techniques and the devotee expresses his devotion to the Guru by service to the local ashram.

The Hare Krishna movement is linked with the Guru, Prabhupada. This, too, is Hindu in its emphasis. Stress is laid on the importance of chanting a 'mantra' as a means of attaining enlightenment. The followers of the cult may be heard chanting the names of God – 'Hare Krishna, Hare Krishna, Krishna, Krishna, Hare, Hare, Hare Rama, Hare Rama, Rama, Rama, Hare, Hare.' It is not unusual to see English young people attired in Indian style dress, the men having their heads shaven apart from a tuft of hair, parading in busy city streets, chanting as they go. This essentially Hindu cult has made an impact on Western young people who have turned their backs on materialism and rationalism.

Transcendental Meditation has been described as a yoga therapy based on the Hindu philosophy of Maharishi Mahesh Yogi. This Indian guru calls the theory behind his teaching

'The Science of Creative Intelligence'. Both his theology and his philosophy are fundamentally Hindu.

The fact is that in the Western world the art of meditation is being learned and this largely as an outcome of the influence of such movements as we have mentioned. Their appeal has mainly been to young people and particularly to the more intelligent.

Other Communities

No mention has been made so far of the Jewish community of some 400,000 living in Britain. This is no new phenomenon. In the Jewish community – as in the Christian – there is an increased secularism coupled with a decline in religious practices. A Jew may be an atheist without impairing his standing as a Jew. It is only if he becomes a Christian or a Muslim that the majority of Jews will question his right to call himself a Jew. As with other ethnic and religious groups, Jews tend to congregate in certain areas such as Stamford Hill, Golders Green and Edgware in north west London, and in Leeds. As with Christians there are liberal and conservative elements among them. Orthodox Jews adhere rigidly to the teaching of the Torah, whilst liberal Jews have been considerably influenced by scientific humanism and higher criticism. There has been for many years a Council for Understanding between Christians and Jews, which has sought to promote dialogue between leaders of the two faiths. In the community generally, Jews in Britain appear to be fully integrated into the world of business and of government, both local and national, as well as in the professions.

In this article, however, we are mainly concerned with those immigrants who have come to Britain in most recent years, especially from the Indian sub-continent and from East Africa, and who represent a non-Christian faith. There are also tens of thousands of West Indians in our midst – they make up Britain's largest coloured minority. They too have their unique dignity and cultural traditions, but for the most part they come from a church background, many with strong pentecostal and fundamentalist roots.

Inter-Faith Dialogue

The somewhat sudden influx of so many men and women from completely different religious and cultural backgrounds found many Christians completely bewildered and unable to cope with the situation. In few areas were local churches sufficiently aware to stretch out a friendly hand to the immigrant community. With the passing years, however, certain tendencies have emerged. In some cases the emphasis has been on inter-faith dialogue with religious leaders, the main aim being to establish good working relationships with those of other faiths. The suggestion has been that we should share our different insights in the hope that thereby we may all come a little nearer to understanding the truth. In Leicester, for example, there is an Inter-Faith Group. From time to time gatherings are arranged for Hindu-Christian dialogue. The genuine aim of such groups is to give Christians and Hindus a deeper understanding of each other's faiths, with a view to achieving a closer relationship between the members of the two communities. In Birmingham the Inter-Faith Council seeks to function as a forum where 'members of the different faiths can meet together in mutual respect and confidence and promote fuller understanding'. This group recently addressed itself to the question of religious education in schools and as a result an Agreed Syllabus has been adopted which is no longer distinctively Christian in its emphasis. Professor John Macquarrie, who has himself paid considerable attention to the relationship between different religions, states that he is not interested in a 'consensus theology' distilled from the religions, but in a 'unity that is coming to be as the religions encounter each other and deepen each other ...' This outlook seems closely akin to that expressed in George Matheson's hymn:

Gather us in, Thou love that fillest all!
Gather our rival faiths within Thy fold!
Rend each man's temple-veil and let it fall,
That we may know that Thou hast been of old;
Gather us in.

Gather us in: we worship only Thee;
In varied names we stretch a common hand;

In diverse forms a common soul to see;
In many ships we seek one spirit-land;
Gather us in.

Each seeks one colour of Thy rainbow-light,
Each looks upon one tint and calls it heaven;
Thou art the fullness of our partial sight;
We are not perfect till we find the seven;
Gather us in.

Thine is the mystic life great India craves,
Thine is the Parsee's sin-destroying beam,
Thine is the Buddhist's rest from tossing waves,
Thine is the empire of vast China's dream;
Gather us in.

Such sentiments do not commend themselves to those who believe that in Christ we have a unique Saviour who occupies a solitary throne. Both indifferentism and syncretism are exceedingly popular today. As W. A. Visser t'Hooft pointed out in his book, 'No Other Name' (SCM Press), even Christians themselves 'give the impression that they consider Christianity as a species of the genus religion, as a sub-division of the general human pre-occupation with the divine.' Earlier in his book, Visser t'Hooft defines the syncretistic approach as 'the view which holds that there is no unique revelation in history, that there are many different ways to reach the divine reality, that all formulations of religious truth or experience are by their very nature inadequate expressions of that truth and that it is necessary to harmonize as much as possible all religious ideas and experiences so as to create one universal religion for mankind.' Such an outlook is far removed from the claims of Christ and New Testament Christianity. In days of unbelief in the western world, some would have us join forces with all the different religions and unitedly face the common enemy, atheism. Neither indifferentism nor syncretism is new to the religious scene. They are continually recurring phenomena. We are constantly being told that there are many ways to God and that God is too great to reveal himself in a single revelation once for all. Yet that is the historic Christian position. We believe that the incarnation was a unique, historical event in which God himself intervened decisively in the world He had created. As Sir Norman Anderson has pointed out in *'Christianity and Comparative Religions'* (Inter Varsity Press): 'In true Christianity, nothing can ever displace the concrete, historical figure of Jesus Christ from the central place.'

Some churches have found themselves in something of a dilemma when a local group of Hindus or Muslims has requested the use of their premises for the holding of services. Needless to say, not all have responded in the same way. A similar dilemma is occasioned when 'Inter-Faith' services are arranged. Christians who take their stand on God's revelation as found in Scripture are almost inevitably going to appear at times as being unco-operative, even intolerant and arrogant. As Sir Norman Anderson observes: 'Neither the Christian Church nor the individual Christian can participate in anything which savours of syncretism . . . the church does not – and must not – apologise for the fact that it regards Jesus Christ as wholly unique.'

Having said this, we do not for one moment suggest there is no place for the study of comparative religion or even for inter-faith dialogue. We do well to know what others believe and to try to understand their culture but we cannot and dare not overlook the uniqueness of the proclamation which is ours to make. That is not to deny that there may be elements of truth in other religions. The fact remains, however, that we have a commission to make known the saving power of Jesus Christ to all men everywhere, since there is no other name whereby men and women may be saved. We need to remind ourselves continually that the human race and the redeemed believer, irrespective of his background, religiously or culturally, is a member of a single new humanity in Christ.

Christian Responsibility

There are, of course, Christians who go beyond inter-faith dialogue and who have a genuine concern to share Christ with their Hindu or Muslim neighbours, as indeed with their disillusioned, materialistically minded neighbours, and friends. They seek to have a positive and evangelistic ministry among immigrants as they speak of 'a mission-field on our doorstep'. One thinks of work such as is being done in Southall, Middlesex: a team effort involving clergy and laity, assisted by some missionaries returned from overseas who have a knowledge of the different languages.

Christians should feel a sense of compassion towards their fellow-men whatever the colour of their skin or whatever their religious faith. We should feel particularly concerned for those who do not perhaps feel at home in our midst. All men everywhere are equally sinners and need Christ. Our concern is to commend the Gospel to those who are lost, whether white or black, and if we are to do this successfully we must study the cultures and thought-patterns of those we are seeking to win. The apostle Paul has clearly pointed the way (1 Cor. 9:19–23). If we are to speak to people in the hope they will listen, we must speak from the position of friendship and in a language which they will understand. God made it clear to his ancient people how they were to regard immigrants: 'When a stranger sojourns with you in your land, you shall not do him wrong. The stranger who sojourns with you shall be to you as the native among you, and you shall love him as yourself; for you were strangers in the land of Egypt: I am the Lord your God' (Lev.19:33f.).

God's standard is that the immigrant in our midst should not be treated as a second-class citizen of Britain and there should be no discriminative action against him. Anything less than that is not just and certainly not biblical.

There is no lack of evidence that racial prejudice is strongly entrenched in certain sections of the community, and even among some Christians. It is our Christian responsibility to show both by our deeds as well as our words that such an attitude is incompatible with the Christian faith.

We must at the same time realise the implications of this. If those adhering to non-Christian faiths are equal citizens with the rest of the community, their rights, including freedom of worship, must be fully respected. It is not easy for Christians, particularly those of the older generation, to come to terms with what it means to live in a pluralistic society such as we have in Britain today.

As the children of an earlier generation of immigrants take their place in our society we must expect to feel increasingly the impact of their presence. More and more frequently we shall see adherents of other faiths being elected to office in local and even national government. It is difficult at this stage to forecast just what long term effect this may have on our educational system and our social services. We must, however, as Christians be ready to accord to our fellow-citizens all the rights and privileges which belong to full citizenship. People of other faiths constitute no more and no less a challenge for evangelization than people of no faith or of only nominal faith.

2

Setting the Scene

MYRTLE S. LANGLEY

'THE TIMES THEY ARE A-CHANGING' – AND THERE IS NO GOING back. This is a fact which Christians in Britain today need not only to accept but to face with understanding, imagination and commitment to the future. In order to do this we must grasp clearly the causes and nature of change and appreciate deeply the effects of change on society as a whole but especially in so far as it has a bearing on religious belief or the lack of it. Only then will we see the need to and be able to formulate and implement 'a Christian approach' to those who profess to belong to one of the many religions, ideologies, sects or cults to be found in pluralist and post-Christian Britain.

1. Shifting Axis

On 4 December 1857 in the Cambridge Senate House, David Livingstone uttered the heroic and now famous words:

> I beg to direct your attention to Africa. I know that in a few years I shall be cut off in that country, which is now open; do not let it be shut again! I go back to Africa to make an open path for commerce and Christianity. Do you carry out the work which I have begun. I leave it with you.

They prompted a burst of applause never surpassed in the building.[1]

That was over a hundred years ago when Christian Britain was at the height of its enthusiasm for civilizing and evangelizing Africa and the rest of the 'heathen' world. Africa is not yet shut. Indeed it could be said that the tables have been turned.

For before our very eyes one of the two or three most significant events in the history of Christianity is taking place. It is nothing less than a change in the centre of gravity of Christianity, so that the heartlands of the church are no longer in Europe, decreasingly in North America, but in South America, in certain parts of Asia and, above all, in Africa.[2]

Take, for example, church growth trends in the twenty-five provinces of the Anglican Communion. Numerical decline is being experienced in Australia, England, Ireland, Scotland, Wales and the United States of America. The number of professing Anglicans remains more or less static in Hong Kong, Brazil, Japan and other parts of South America. In marked contrast converts are being gained rapidly in Central Africa, Kenya, Papua/New Guinea, Sudan, Tanzania and Uganda. Moreover, contrary to the normal pattern in Anglicanism of baptizing more infants than adults Kenya and Uganda, in 1977, baptized more adults than infants.[3]

It is therefore not without justification that church leaders in the Third World call for a moratorium on missionaries from the Older Churches and expect to assume leadership in the church of tomorrow.[4]

Certainly, it is from the living, growing Churches of the Third World that the most creative theology has come in the last two decades. While Christians in the Older Churches are traversing yet again the well-trodden path of christological controversy (the *Myth of God Incarnate* and all that) Christians in the Newer Churches are being constrained to think through and live out their faith in terms of their own cultural and socio-political contexts. We are engaged in ivory-tower debate, they are doing theology at grass-roots level. From South America comes the *theology of liberation* where the emphasis is on faith in action and from Africa come exciting developments in *liturgical renewal*.[5]

2. Changing World

Says Alvin Toffler in his book *Future Shock*:

It has been observed that if the last 50,000 years of man's existence were divided into lifetimes of approximately 62 years

each, there have been about 800 such lifetimes. Of these 800, fully
650 were spent in caves. Only during the last 70 lifetimes has it
been possible to communicate effectively from one lifetime to
another – as writing made it possible to do. Only during the last
six lifetimes did masses of men ever see a printed word. Only
during the last four has it been possible to measure time with any
precision. Only in the last two has anyone anywhere used an
electric motor. And the overwhelming majority of all the material
goods we use in daily life today have been developed within the
present, the 800th, lifetime.[6]

Thus he conveys dramatically the immensity of the technological revolution which must be regarded as the second great
break in the history of mankind after the invention of agricul-
ture. It has given rise to a variety of new and complex situations and has evoked conflicting and ambivalent responses.

The affluent society arrived (for some). The global village
was created (by others). Nothing seemed unfeasible in the
early sixties. Technology promised an open future. Great possibilities seemed to lie ahead in terms of economic planning,
population control and direction, medical research, development and social projection. Hope was abroad.

Then disillusionment set in. In the late sixties stories of
protest, violence, terror and world shortages of food, energy
and non-renewable resources dominated the world news.
Ecological awareness began to cry out for a more simple life
style; global consciousness started taking note that two thirds
of the world's population lived on or below the bread line.

Christians in Britain, no less than everyone else, find themselves caught on the horns of this dilemma. Moreover, they are
also faced with yet further consequences of the technological
revolution. They belong to a society which has been in turn
industrialized, urbanized, collectivised and depersonalized by
technology. For the majority this has meant alienation, not
only from God, the ground of their being, but from their
fellow humans, the rest of creation and the work of their
hands. In short, it has meant dehumanization. Life has come
to have neither purpose nor meaning and work no longer
fulfils. For many this has resulted either in taking refuge in an
ideology such as Marxism or in seeking solace and fulfilment
in some form of religion. As a recent commentator puts it:

24

> There is a resurgence of religion (often in unconventional forms), with a hunger for awe and wonder and holiness, for imagination and the non-rational, for silence, for personal experience and individuality, for the disciplines of spiritual formation.[7]

Unfortunately, she concludes, these are seldom readily available in the Churches and people turn elsewhere – to witchcraft and the occult, to eastern mysticism and to life in community.

3. Conflicting Cultures

In the course of thirty years Britain has lost an empire and gained a commonwealth of nations, exchanged imperial prosperity for membership of the European Economic Community and been transformed from a Christian nation to a pluralistic society. All three have had far-reaching consequences but the first and the last are particularly relevant to our purposes. Decolonization has led to an influx of coloured immigrants into Britain and therefore to the formation of a multiracial, multicultural and multireligious society.

These immigrants left home ostensibly for two reasons: they were recruited for the post-war labour market or driven from home by economic or political necessity. In the former category fall West Indians brought over by British firms in the fifties, and in the latter East African Asians with British passports forced out by independent African governments in the sixties, and Indians and Pakistanis lured by better prospects in Britain.

All brought with them distinctive religious and social customs. From India, Pakistan and East Africa have come Muslims, Hindus and Sikhs, and from the West Indies Christians not only belonging to the historic or mainstream Churches but to the relatively modern and experiential pentecostal movement.

As 'natives' and 'immigrants' meet, cultural differences become only too apparent, particularly those relating to family structures, relationships and discipline, marriage customs and religious practices. This is only natural, but differences of race serve to heighten the contrast. Both groups begin to feel insecure and threatened. In addition, the situation is exploited by political opportunists and prophets of doom.

However, for Christians there is only one way forward: to ascertain the facts of the matter and then set our faces towards living and working together in equality and harmony. The facts speak for themselves.

The Office of Population Censuses and Surveys estimates that in mid-1976 there were 1,771,000 coloured people (including those of mixed descent) in the United Kingdom. This represented 3.3 per cent of the population or fewer than four out of every 100 people. According to a report published by the Central Statistical Office in January 1977 this population could grow by 5 per cent per year in the next ten years. This would mean a coloured population of 2,656,000 in the mid-1980s or (providing the rest of the population does not increase) 4.7 per cent of the total or fewer than five out of every 100 people.[8]

4. Declining Faith?

In Britain today historic or mainstream Christianity is in rapid decline, whereas other religions, ideologies, sects and cults are gaining in strength. Admittedly some, but by no means all, of the latter is due to immigration.

Some measure of Christianity's decline and the devaluation of organized religion may be gained by examining the institutional Churches' numerical strength and socio-political influence and the relative decline in rewards of the clergy.

Firstly, let us take numerical strength. The National Census of England and Wales taken in 1851 revealed that on a representative Sunday in that year 45 per cent of the population attended church. The Evangelical Alliance Survey published in 1978 estimates that in 1975 18.2 per cent or 7,850,000 of Britain's population were active members of Britain's Christian churches. Between the years 1970 and 1975 there had been an overall decline of 2 per cent or 650,000. However, it is the historic or mainstream denominations which are in decline while some independent and most small, holiness, pentecostal and ethnic together with the Lutherans and the Orthodox are experiencing growth. So too are the sects and cults, up from 260,000 in 1970 to 305,870 in 1975, and all the other religions (Buddhists, Hindus, Muslims, Sikhs, School of Meditation), up from 383,821 in 1970 to 639,862 in 1975, except the Jews, down from 113,000 in 1970 to 111,000 in 1975. On the other hand, if we are to judge strength by community religious adherence then the nation is still 68 per cent Christian – 38,100,000 out of a total of 56 million people.[9]

Secondly, let us take socio-political influence. Bryan Wilson, the Oxford sociologist of religion, avers that since 1952 when G. Stephens Spinks and his two collaborators in *Religion in Britain since 1900* 'picked their way dolefully among the evidences of the steady decay of institutional religion in search of occasional signs of possible hope' the Churches have become even more completely separate compartments of the British social system:

> Religious attitudes penetrate less and less effectively into social activities and individual lives; and the involvement of individuals in religious practice has become more emphatically a matter of private, individual choice.
> Except under the ancient protocol of solemn processions, the church has now ceased to exercise even nominal presidency over our national life. A Prime Minister's correspondence 80 years ago dealt seriously with archiepiscopal opinion; 40 years ago the bishops had a significant voice in the abdication crisis; today, we have even seen the occasion when the Prime Minister was 'too busy' to see the Archbishop of Canterbury. The mass media have virtually eclipsed the pulpit as a source of information and guidance. Armies of specialists now fulfil the educational, counselling, rehabilitative, and pastoral functions that were once the virtual monopoly of the clergy, or their religiously approved lay agents.
> Religion itself is no longer news, except when a clergyman commits a moral misdemeanour, or when exorcism or the occult is involved. Convocations, assemblies, and synods are not now worth the cost of newsprint . . .[10]

Thirdly, let us take the decline in the relative rewards of the clergy. Even in the fifties the clergy shared something of the material and cultural standards and the social status of the professional classes. Today they are among the lowest paid. Even unskilled manual workers earn considerably more. Society rewards according to its evaluation of the work. It appears that today the clergy are, in the words of Wilson, 'merely amateur helpers, and British society rewards them as such'.[11]

In addition to taking note of Christian decline we might do well to contemplate resurgent Islam, demonstrated most recently by the launching in December 1977 of a £1 million missionary crusade to Christians by the Ahmadiyya movement, and by the plans for the erection of the Aga Khan's Ismaili movement's headquarters on a site alongside the Victoria and Albert Museum in Kensington, London.[12]

5. Secularizing Influences

Ghosts from the nineteenth century still haunt us in the present. Many of our presuppositions – at least concerning religion – are based on theories formulated in the past. Men like Darwin and Müller, Marx, Durkheim and Freud continue to exert secularizing influences on our present world. Their views about evolution and religion still undergird much that is taught in the physical and social sciences and in the comparative study of religion.

In the field of *religion* it all began with the publication of Charles Darwin's (1809–82) *The Origin of Species* in 1859 and continued with the tireless efforts of Friedrich Max Müller (1823–1900), epitomized in his massive compendium *Sacred Books of the East*. In Darwinism scientific theory joined hands with a dominant philosophy of history and embraced evolution as the guiding principle of method – a principle adopted and applied with assiduity and vigour in the field of religion. In Müller foundations were laid in the Western world for the dialogue of religions lately come into its own. Moreover, that God may be considered dead, man come of age and religion abolished is evolutionary theory in practice.[13]

In the fields of *sociology and psychology* as related to religion, Karl Marx (1818–83), Émile Durkheim (1858–1917) and Sigmund Freud (1856–1939) propounded functional theories of religion, influential in their time and still very much with us. Religion, so they asserted, is functional to social cohesion and solidarity.

Marx, as early as 1843–4, when he was only twenty-five or

thereabouts, addressed himself to the subject of religion in some brilliant epigrams:

> Religion is indeed the self-consciousness and self-esteem of man who has either not yet won through to himself or has already lost himself again ... It is the fantastic realization of the human essence since the human essence has not acquired any true reality
> ...
> Religious suffering is at one and the same time the expression of real suffering and a protest against real suffering. Religion is the sigh of the oppressed creature, the heart of a heartless world and the soul of soulless circumstances. It is the opium of the people.
> The abolition of religion as the illusory happiness of the people is the demand for their real happiness. To call on them to give up their illusions about their condition is to call on them to give up a condition that requires illusions. The criticism of religion is therefore in embryo the criticism of that vale of tears of which religion is the halo.[14]

To summarise, religion legitimates for the economic and political state of the poor and oppressed, offering compensation for deprivation in fantasies of an after life.

Durkheim (still influential in the sociology of religion) in *The Elementary Forms of the Religious Life* examined Australian totemism as the simplest and most original form of religion, and concluded:

> Religious beliefs rest upon a specific experience whose demonstrative value is, in one sense, not one bit inferior to that of scientific experiments, though different from them ... But from the fact that a 'religious experience', if we choose to call it this, does exist and that it has a certain foundation – and, by the way, is there any experience which has none? – it does not follow that the reality which is its foundation conforms objectively to the idea which believers have of it ...
> We have seen that this reality, which mythologies have represented under so many different forms, but which is the universal and eternal objective cause of these sensations *sui generis* out of which religious experience is made, is society. We have shown what moral forms it develops and how it awakens this sentiment of a refuge, of a shield and of a guardian support which attaches the believer to his cult. It is that which raises him outside himself; it is even that which made him ...
> Religious forces are therefore human forces, moral forces.[15]

In sum, Durkheim believed that society deifies itself so that in effect it can be equated with God. Society virtually is God.

Freud is known as the father of depth psychology, or modern psychoanalysis, but his influence in the sphere of religion has been of considerable importance. Basically he believed religion to be a projection of infantile dependencies – an illusion – and the history of religion to be the history of a collective neurosis:

> As we ... know, the terrifying impression of helplessness in childhood aroused the need for protection – for protection through love – which was provided by the father; and the recognition that this helplessness lasts throughout life made it necessary to cling to the existence of a father, but this time a more powerful one. Thus the benevolent rule of a divine Providence allays our fear of the dangers of life; the establishment of a moral world-order ensures the fulfilment of the demands of justice, which have so often remained unfulfilled in human civilization; and the prolongation of earthly existence in a future life provides the local and temporal framework in which these wish-fulfilments shall take place ...
>
> When I say that these things are all illusions, I must define the meaning of the word. An illusion is not the same thing as an error; nor is it necessarily an error ... What is characteristic of illusions is that they are derived from human wishes. In this respect they come near to psychiatric delusions. But they differ from them, too ... Illusions need not necessarily be false – that is to say, unrealizable or in contradiction to reality ... Thus we call a belief an illusion when a wish-fulfilment is a prominent factor in its motivation, and in doing so we disregard its relations to reality, just as the illusion itself sets no store by verification ...
>
> Having thus taken our bearings, let us return once more to the question of religious doctrines. We can now repeat that all of them are illusions and insusceptible of proof.[16]

All three, Marx, Durkheim and Freud, ignored the supernatural in religion. Many of their successors do likewise although there are welcome signs of a rediscovery of the supernatural.[17]

6. Continuing Crisis

The crisis is one of identity. Just *who* are we? A concept

familiar to anthropologists is that of the *rite de passage*, a ritual carried out to mark the transition from one state in life to another (for example, childhood to adulthood, unmarried to married). During such a rite there occurs a transitional or *liminal* phase, when the person being initiated occupies a 'betwixt and between' position; when having lost his former status he has not yet acquired a new one.

Recently this has been applied to liminal periods of history, when old structures are passing away and a new social order has not yet taken shape. Ours is such a period. To belong to our society is to be 'in transit', neither here nor there, without position or place.

In rites of passage a specific type of community emerges: it has no internal authority structure; the members are simply 'in transit' and submit themselves to the general authority of the ritual elders. This community state or *communitas* can also be seen, it is suggested, during liminal periods of history. Now there are certain attributes of the 'transition community' in a rite of passage which bear a striking resemblance to those that can be distinguished in 'liminal' periods of history. They include: absence of property, reduction of all to the same status level, the wearing of uniform apparel (or nakedness), sexual continence (or its antithesis, sexual community), minimization of sex distinctions, obliteration of rank, humility, disregard for personal appearance, unselfishness, total obedience to the prophet or leader, sacred instruction, the maximization of religious as opposed to secular attitudes and behaviour, suspension of kinship rights and obligations, simplicity of speech and manners, sacred folly, acceptance of pain and suffering, and so forth.[18]

Without much difficulty or imagination we can recognize attributes of manifestations known to us from past and present: monks, nuns and mendicants (such as the Franciscans), millenarian movements (such as the Jehovah's Witnesses), brotherhoods (such as the Exclusive Brethren) and communities or communes, Christian and non-Christian, prevalent in Western Europe and America during the sixties and seventies (such as the Greenbus Community in Glastonbury, the Findhorn Foundation in Moray, the more widely known Children of God, Jesus Family and hippies). One writer estimates that some one hundred communal ventures of various kinds were to be found in Britain in 1972.[19]

This sort of 'liminal' *communitas* is not permanent of course. Whether in a rite of passage or in a liminal period of history it will be replaced by structured relationships. (Although one can distinguish some instances of permanent liminality such as monastic orders.) But as we await the development of such structures, we may reflect that liminal periods of history turn up fertile soil in which to sow the seeds of the gospel. That soil includes those of other faiths in Britain; moreover, these people remain very much on the margins of our society. It is our Christian duty and privilege to bring them in.

NOTES

1 Geoffrey Moorhouse, *The Missionaries*, London, Eyre Methuen, 1973, pp. 19, 131.
2 A. F. Walls, 'Towards Understanding Africa's Place in Christian History' in J. S. Pobee (ed.), *Religion in a Pluralistic Society*, Leiden, E. J. Brill, 1976, pp. 180–81.
3 Tom Tuma, 'Directions in Church Growth' in John Howe (ed.), *Today's Church and Today's World: The Lambeth Conference 1978 Preparatory Articles*, London, CIO, 1977, pp. 96–7.
4 Ibid, p. 102.
5 For example, see Gustavo Gutiérrez, *A Theology of Liberation*, London, SCM, 1974; M.-L. Martin, *Kimbangu*, Oxford, Blackwell, 1975.
6 Quoted in Hans Küng, *On Being a Christian*, London, Collins, 1977, pp. 38–9.
7 Margaret Dewey, 'Dominant Influences in the Current World' in John Howe (ed.), op. cit., p. 52.
8 *The Guardian Weekly*, Vol. 118, No. 7, February 12, 1978, p. 10.
9 Peter Brierley (compiler), *UK Protestant Missions Handbook Volume 2: Home*, London, Evangelical Alliance, 1977 pp. 7 ff., 10 ff., 13 ff. (The Jewish figures have been questioned.)
10 Bryan Wilson, 'How Religious Are We?' in *New Society*, Vol. 42, No. 786, 27 October 1977, pp. 176–8.
11 Ibid.
12 Reported respectively in the *Church Times*, No. 5991, December 9, 1977 and *The Times*, February 4, 1978.
13 Cf. Eric J. Sharpe, *Comparative Religion: A History*, London, Duckworth, 1975, pp. 25–6, 35–46.
14 Karl Marx, 'A Contribution to the Critique of Hegel's Philosophy of Right: Introduction' in e.g. David McLellan (ed.), *Karl*

Marx: Selected Writings, Oxford, OUP, 1977 or Colletti – Livingstone – Benton, *Karl Marx: Early Writings* (The Pelican Marx Library), Harmondsworth, Penguin, 1975.

15 Émile Durkheim, *The Elementary Forms of the Religious Life*, London, Allen and Unwin, 1915, pp. 417–19.

16 Sigmund Freud, *The Future of an Illusion*, London, Hogarth Press, 1962, pp. 26–9.

17 For example see sociologist Peter Berger's *A Rumour of Angels: Modern Society and the Rediscovery of the Supernatural*, Harmondsworth, Penguin, 1970. *New Society's* reviewer stated 'This little book, vigorous and authoritative, could mark an important turning-point in twentieth-century thought'.

18 Victor W. Turner, *The Ritual Process*, London, Routledge, 1969, pp. 94–165.

19 Cf. Andrew Lockley, *Christian Communes*, London, SCM, 1976 and David Clark, *Basic Communities*, London, SPCK, 1977.

Part Two

A Christian Approach

3

Our Lord's Approaches to People of Other Cultures[1]

MAURICE HOBBS

'CHRISTIAN APPROACHES TO PEOPLE OF OTHER FAITHS' IN Britain today must surely be modelled upon the words and practice of the Founder of our faith: the Lord Jesus himself.

Our Saviour was born a Jew and he knew, even if he did not sympathise with, Jewish attitudes towards people of other ethnic groups ('ethnic' is derived from the Greek *ethnos*, translated 'Gentiles' in the New Testament). He knew, as St. John thought it necessary to explain to his readers, that 'Jews and Samaritans, ... do not use vessels in common'. He sent out the apostles on their mission with the following instructions: 'Do not take the road to Gentile lands and do not enter any Samaritan town' (Matt. 10.5). When he encountered the Canaanite woman (Matt. 15.21), he told her that he 'was sent to the lost sheep of the house of Israel and to them alone', and Israel He called 'the children', while the outsiders were 'dogs'!

From the Old Testament, the national literature of his people, the Lord Jesus knew the many stories of contact and conflict with other cults and cultures and the unending struggle to maintain religious (and biological?) purity – for instance, the destruction of the Midianites after the affair of Zimri and Cozbi (Numbers 25 and 31); the conquest of the Promised Land and the prohibition of intermarriage with its inhabitants (Deut. 7:1–6); and the consternation recorded in Ezra (9.2ff) when it was realised that 'the holy race has become mixed with the foreign population'.

On the other hand, he would also have known the alternative strand in the self-recognition of Israel as the people of

God, through whom blessings would come to Gentiles. The story of Ruth, his own Moabite ancestor, tells of the way love breaks down ethnic barriers. It is unlikely that his mother did not tell him of the words of Simeon, about 'a light to lighten the Gentiles', which themselves echo Isaiah's prophecy (42:6) about the Servant of the Lord, 'appointed to be a light to all peoples, a beacon for the nations'. Childhood experiences, like that visit of the 'three wise men from the East', or the flight into Egypt, will surely have been seen as relevant to other people and other places.

If Matthew could open his Gospel simply with: 'This is the story of the birth of the Messiah' (Matt. 1:18), surely 'Jesus Christ, Son of David, Son of Abraham' was aware that he stood in the main stream of Jewish history and expectation. From that point of view, he must also have been aware of the realities of power for a subject people, under the rule of the Edomite Herods, puppets of the Roman Emperor. It was probably common knowledge in his family that Anna, the prophetess, 'talked about the child to all who were looking for the liberation of Jerusalem (Luke 2:38). His disciples certainly 'had been hoping that he was the man to liberate Israel' (Luke 24:21), while 'the presence of a Zealot (or past Zealot) among the apostles gives rise to interesting speculation' (F. F. Bruce in *New Bible Dictionary*, under 'Cananaean'). Christians in Britain today who wish to make approaches to people of other faiths must also be aware of the political realities which fashion their lives.

All this from a human point of view – but the Person in whom the twin concepts of Messiah and Suffering Servant of the Lord blended, made the great universal statement: 'God loved the world so much that he gave his only begotten Son, that everyone who has faith in him may not die but have eternal life' (John 3:16 NEB), so putting to an end the exclusive possessiveness of Jewish understandings of God, and laying the foundations of a 'single new humanity in himself' (Ephesians 2:15 NEB).

Within the social setting of his time and country, the Lord Jesus set about establishing the ground rules of that new humanity, a process that can be illuminated by his relations with people of other ethnic groups. It is the purpose of this paper to examine his actions and social relations with them and what he said to, and about, them.

Jesus and Samaritans

In spite of his instructions to the Apostles Jesus did not confine himself to areas where he might meet only Jews. 'He went and settled at Capernaum on the Sea of Galilee', Galilee 'of the Gentiles' (Matt. 4:12,15): 'He withdrew to the region of Tyre and Sidon' and 'He had to pass through Samaria' (John 4:4).

What is more, the 'Samaritans ... pressed him to stay with them; and he stayed there two days', which means that he broke the taboos upon social intercourse – the use of cooking and eating vessels. It was not for nothing that later 'the Jews answered, "Are we not right in saying that you are a Samaritan and that you are possessed?" ' (John 8:48), but it is significant that though he repudiated the charge of demon possession, he did not refuse the label of 'Samaritan'.

As Son of Man and Saviour of the World, he could hardly have done so. As members of 'his Body, belonging to the single new humanity' can his present day followers do less than go where the modern 'Samaritans' are, break the taboos upon social intercourse and accept the label? Many Christians honour the name of Hudson Taylor, who went 'to live entirely alone among the Chinese', learned the 'Shanghai dialect', and adopted Chinese dress and hairstyle (see Dr. and Mrs. Howard Taylor: *Hudson Taylor in Early Years*). That was in the 1850's, more than a century ago, and in China, more than 5,000 miles away. The mission-field, for many of us, is in our own town and street.

What the Lord Jesus said to and about Samaritans is also significant. His opportunity to speak with the woman at the well arose out of his weariness and thirst: and the conversation continued about real issues such as her marriage and intercultural misunderstandings and about the time when the worship and knowledge of God would transcend its traditional expression, whether in Jerusalem or through Gerizim. The conversation ended in disclosure: 'I am He (The Messiah)' said Jesus. Perhaps it is in conversation, human and real, with people of other ethnic groups in the inner city, that the Body of Christ will disclose itself for what it is.

The Lord Jesus also told a story (Luke 10:25–37), the hero of which was a Samaritan, whose compassion broke through 'the enmity which stood like a dividing wall' (Eph. 2:14) between Samaritans and Jews. In the story, the priest and levite, distinguished from other men by their function and their sanctity, failed at the point of real, individual need. Their reaction to the half-dead victim was presumably controlled by regulations like those in Leviticus 21:11 and Numbers 6:9 which required ritual separation and purification after contact with the dead, and would have prevented them from performing their temple duties.

In contrast, the Samaritan traveller was distinguished by his membership of the minority group of mixed race (Nehemiah 13) of unorthodox faith and defective ritual. Yet it was he who touched the wounded man, and arranged for his continuing care, regardless of his own convenience.

The story was Christ's answer to the question 'Who is my neighbour?', and the lawyer who asked it was forced to acknowledge that 'the one who showed kindness' was the neighbour. 'Jesus said, "Go and do as he did". Behave like a Samaritan?' No, behave like one in whom love is in action; like a member of the 'single new humanity ... thereby making peace'.

Following His Example

The relations between the Lord Jesus and the ethnic groups of his time are, I think, highly significant for his followers in Britain today:

1. Approaches cross-culturally arose out of real situations of need: his weariness and thirst and the predicament of the robbers' victim. There is a real problem here in the relatively high status and wealth of most white Christians over against the people of other ethnic groups in this country, but there are plenty of real situations requiring dialogue. For instance, between parents and teachers about the under-achievement of 'immigrant' children: between Christian employers and parents about the special difficul-

ties of black school-leavers in finding and keeping jobs:
between black and white churches about their segregation
and the deployment and use of capital resources, buildings,
etc. It is interesting to see in Jesus' conversation at the well
how naturally attention turned from social matters, to the
underlying theology, whereas our practice seems to begin
with theological statements.

2. Intercourse was not merely verbal and public, but the Lord
   Jesus stayed two days in Sychar and the good Samaritan at
   least one night at the inn. This involved close physical
   proximity, sharing of facilities, the destruction of social
   controls that keep individuals and communities apart.
   Members of 'the body of Christ', the 'single new humanity'
   will want to experience what it means to be 'incorporate in
   Christ', across ethnic boundaries. To do so may mean not
   only occasional visits to other people's homes, but genuine
   attempts to live in community; to learn and use in public
   worship as well as ordinary conversations languages other
   than English: to add one more consideration when moving
   home – 'Where can we have fellowship with Chinese or
   West Indian or Asian Christians?'

3. The Lord Jesus used the deeds of the good Samaritan in
   almost explicit criticism of Judaism. How far could we go
   in parallel criticism of Christian practice, in the light of
   Islam or Hinduism? It would, of course, be possible to say
   that the good Samaritan transcended his culture, but he
   must have been formed within it. That one such individual
   appeared (the realism of the details of the story suggests
   that it actually happened) warns us against block stereo-
   typing – they are *not* 'all the same'.

4. Jesus maintained the perspective of the Messiah, leader of a
   new order, throughout: a new scale of values, a new loyalty, over and above both Judaism and Samaritan religion.
   'God is Spirit', he said, to be worshipped in spirit and in
   truth, not merely in Jerusalem or on Mt. Gerizim (John 4).
   It is from this point of view, that members of the 'new
   humanity in himself' will approach inter-faith and cross

cultural contacts. All 'folk' or 'civil' religion, whether Jewish or Samaritan, came under scrutiny.

NOTES

1 Adapted from an article entitled 'Ethnic groups in the Life of Our Lord Jesus Christ' in the Journal of the Evangelical Race Relations Group, Vol. 1. No. 3. Sept/Oct. 1975.

4

Christianity, Truth and Dialogue

KENNETH G. HOWKINS

'CHRISTIAN' WAS THE NAME COINED IN SYRIAN ANTIOCH IN THE first century for the disciples of the Lord Jesus Christ. It may have been a nickname, but it was quite appropriate, as these people were always talking about Christ, who had evidently made a tremendous impression on them. The account of the situation in which this name arose (Acts 11:19–26) gives an indication of its significance. Some believers were 'preaching the Lord Jesus'. We could translate this as 'preaching the Gospel, that Jesus is the Lord'. When Barnabas, an envoy from Jerusalem, saw that people believed, he recognized this as 'the grace of God', and he himself is described as 'full of the Holy Spirit'. So in the beginning the term 'Christian' was associated with God and his grace, Jesus as Lord, and the Holy Spirit.

Eighteen centuries later, Kierkegaard, a Danish philosopher and theologian, made the caustic comment that in his day the term 'Christian' was applied to everybody, so that to be human was to be Christian. He added that a determinant was a word that pointed out some determining characteristic; so that if the term 'Christian' was used of everyone, it was no longer a determinant, and no longer had any meaning. That warning is still relevant.

Today 'Christian' is given such a wide range of meanings, that even those who deny a major part of what the term originally involved still adhere to the name. They would claim that they are holding to what Christianity really is or should be, at the present time. They would claim too that what they are rejecting is solely what is outmoded or unacceptable in the light of our present knowledge.

Evangelical Christians claim to adhere to apostolic Christianity as witnessed to in the New Testament. This is their guide and standard in faith and practice. Of course the New Testament is not a theological handbook. It is a handbook to faith and life. Theology is a systematic organization of what is presented in the New Testament in a different form. Theology is the theory behind the religion. Thus when the evangelical Christian is considering his approach to other religions, he may not find a neat and ready-made answer in the New Testament. The answer has to be thought out. So he seeks a theological basis for his approach to other religions. This theological basis is within the very nature of Christianity itself and the Christian message.

As the name implies, and as Paul directly asserts (1 Cor. 3:11), the foundation of Christianity is Christ himself, or, to give him his full title, the Lord Jesus Christ. Each term in this title is significant. He is Lord, or Ruler, just as God himself is also called Lord. He is Jesus, identified with a particular human being. He is Christ, the Anointed, or the Messiah, the One sent by God and awaited by the Jewish people.

The Message of Jesus

First we must go back to the message of Jesus himself. Central to this was his teaching about the Kingdom of God. He proclaimed that the Kingdom, or Rule, or Reign, of God was beginning. Of course, in one sense God always had been ruling, and when God created man in his own image, giving him the power to choose, God did not abandon his sovereign control. The Old Testament illustrates constantly that 'the Most High rules in the kingdom of men' (Dan. 4:25), whatever men may do. But now God was setting up his Kingdom in a new way. Entering the Kingdom meant accepting the Rule of God, and that involved repentance, or a total change.

But Jesus Christ did not only proclaim the coming of the Kingdom: He was himself vitally connected with the Kingdom. His words and deeds showed that God was at work, and he acted with God's authority, even forgiving sins, which was the prerogative of God alone. It was quite clear that Jesus was a genuine man, but it also became apparent that Jesus could not be explained solely in human terms. He tended to avoid titles which would easily be misunderstood, but he did use the title Son of Man (Dan. 7:13), thus claiming to be the Leader and Representative of God's people. As God's Representative with God's authority, he claimed that men's eternal destiny would be determined by their attitude towards him (Mark 8:38). He addressed God as his Father in a unique way; he was recognized by the early Christians as being the Son of God.

Thus Jesus shared in the very Being of God, as well as the being of man. When we speak of the Incarnation we mean thus that the eternal Son of God became man. Jesus was not just a godly man: he was the God-man. It is all too easy to stress part of the truth and to ignore another part. Some Christians stress Jesus' deity, and pay little attention to his humanity. This may be in part a reaction, and also in part a result of paying more attention to the epistles in the New Testament than to the Gospels.

The humanity of Jesus was real. He lived as we live; he endured temptation, suffering and weakness; he was genuinely one of us. The New Testament constantly shows Jesus' full humanity. Because of this, he can sympathize with us, be our example, and represent us before God. Because of his humanity, he has something which all men have; he shares the humanity of all men. This is a vital part of the significance of Jesus.

The importance of the cross is seen in the amount of space which the Gospels devote to the events leading up to the crucifixion, and to the crucifixion itself. Paul claimed that his message was just 'Jesus Christ and him crucified' (1 Cor. 2:2). The essence of the Christian explanation of the crucifixion of Jesus is that it was 'for our sins' (1 Cor. 15:3). Moreover, it was 'for the sins of the whole world' (1 John 2:2). Thus in his life and in his death Jesus has universal significance.

But the message of Christianity does not stop there. God raised Jesus from the dead, and the resurrection is fundamental. Without it there would be no Christ now, no salvation, and no church. By the resurrection, Jesus was shown to be the Son of God with power (Rom. 1:4). He always was God's Son: now this was demonstrated with power.

The Message of the Early Church

The preaching in the early church illustrates the essential content of the Christian message. The story of the life, death and resurrection of Jesus was told, and this was related to the Old Testament. It was shown that God had acted in Christ, and brought salvation through him. Such was the message to Jews, and they were urged to see that all their hopes and expectations were fulfilled in Jesus.

When the Christian message was proclaimed to Gentiles, that is, to non-Jews with a different background, Paul was the foremost preacher. He reshaped the message, using different language, but without changing the essential content. Central to his thinking was not so much the Kingdom, or Reign, of God, as the Righteousness of God. In fact Paul declares that God's righteousness is revealed in the gospel (Rom. 1:16).

In the first place, righteousness was an attribute of God himself, and God demanded righteousness, as the Old Testament prophets had said. But the concept of righteousness goes further. God, acting in righteousness, delivered the oppressed, so that his righteousness included 'setting things right'. This process had begun in Old Testament times, and the climax was anticipated in the future Messianic Age. God had already worked mightily in Christ, and this was interpreted as the beginning of the Messianic Age, now dawning. If Paul's language referred more to the righteousness of God than to the Kingdom of God, the meaning was ultimately the same. For if a man was justified, or counted righteous, by God, because of Christ, he was restored to a right relationship with God, or reconciled, and that in turn meant that he acknowledged God as his King and Ruler. Righteousness was to be an attribute of the Christian. His character was to be transformed. That was part of the salvation brought by Christ, and effected in man by the Holy Spirit.

Paul's view of Christ was as lofty as it could possibly be. He even used Old Testament language which described God, and applied it to Jesus (Phil. 2:9–11). Jesus Christ was exalted above all powers, natural and supernatural, physical and spiritual, temporal and eternal. His name was the highest of all. So Christ was for all people; there was no room for another as he was the greatest; all nations could now become members of the 'chosen race', in Christ. Christ was the sole mediator between God and man (1 Tim. 2:5), so that over against Jewish and Gentile religion, 'There is one God ... and one Lord Jesus Christ' (1 Cor. 8:5–6).

Hope is a basic element in Christianity. Jesus Christ himself taught about the beginning of the Kingdom and its consummation. Throughout the New Testament we find the hope of the return, or second coming, of Christ. But the Christian hope is not set solely in the next world. There is also an 'intermediate hope'. Just as Jesus cared for both the physical and the spiritual well-being of people, so should the Christian. There are social dimensions to Christianity, and social implications. This is not to equate the Gospel with social concern, but to include the here and now, as well as the hereafter, in the Christian's purview.

Christian Beliefs

As was said earlier, when the term 'Christian' was first coined, it was associated with God, Jesus Christ and the Holy Spirit. The first disciples were Jews who were ardently monotheistic: they were certain that there was only one God. Without changing that belief, they came to see Jesus Christ as (somehow) God, and they knew and experienced God as they knew Jesus. To see Jesus was to see God (John 14:9). Jesus made God real to them. Similarly, when the Holy Spirit was given at Pentecost, he made Jesus real and ever-present to the disciples, and thus also made God real and present. He was the Spirit of God and the Spirit of Jesus.

Although the actual word 'Trinity' is not used in the New Testament, the idea is there. The experience and belief of the Christians was such that when it was thought out and formulated theologically, the doctrine of the Trinity arose. This is not to say that there was a new doctrine formed, but rather that when Christians considered what they knew of God, of Jesus Christ, and of the Holy Spirit, the only way they could express it was by this term 'Trinity'. God was known and experienced as Three, but God was still One. Hence the Tri-unity, or Trinity.

In Christian belief, God is Trinity in his own Being, in himself. In other words, while the doctrine of the Trinity is the way to express Christian experience of God, it is not solely a convenient way of describing experience, nor of describing what God appears to be; rather it describes what God actually is himself. It may be argued that God cannot be known as he is in himself, but only as he reveals himself. To this it may be answered that God has revealed himself as Trinity. We must look at the significance of this.

God is transcendent, that is, over and above, outside and beyond, his creation. Creation, this world, and we ourselves, are not part of God (as pantheists say), but are separate from him, and dependent on him. This is seen in the opening verses of the Bible. But in this same passage (if this is a correct translation) the Spirit of God 'moved over the face of the waters'. Here God is immanent, that is, in, with, among his creation and creatures. These two attributes of God, held together, keep us from either deism, which sees God as entirely outside his creation, or pantheism, which sees God as entirely in his creation. Instead we have theism: God separate from, but acting in, his creation.

Now this is the constant view of the Old Testament. But with the New Testament comes the fulness of God's revelation of himself. God is not only Father and Holy Spirit, but also Son. Moreover, this Son is identified with one, actual, historical human being, Jesus of Nazareth. The witness of the New Testament is not that God adopted, or appointed, this man as his Son, but that God sent his pre-existing Son into this world.

This definite and particular revelation of God in his Son is the climax of previous revelation. God was not just vaguely 'God', but 'The God of Abraham'. He was not just transcendent and unknown, nor just immanent and vaguely known, but known particularly and definitely. It was from this background of revelation that Jesus Christ came, as 'the Word made flesh'. Thus God did not enter humanity in general, in becoming flesh, but in one particular human being, Jesus of Nazareth. Moreover, this incarnation, or 'becoming flesh', was viewed both as the climax of past revelation in Judaism, and as the final revelation, as nothing more remained to be revealed. The finality is seen not only in the revelation which

Jesus Christ brought, or rather, *was*, but more especially in his death, which was the once-for-all atonement for sin.

It will be clear from this that there is a special relationship between Judaism and Christianity. Judaism prepared the way for Christ and Christianity; Christ fulfilled and superseded Judaism. The continuing revelation of God in Judaism was completed in Christ: God, who previously had spoken little by little, in various ways, to the fathers by the prophets, has spoken by a Son (Heb. 1:1-2). Also the animal sacrifices of Judaism and all the rituals, which were a temporary way of dealing with sin, have been fulfilled, replaced and outmoded by Christ, whose eternal sacrifice of himself has achieved perfectly and in reality what Jewish sacrifices achieved imperfectly and as a shadow of reality (as the Epistle to the Hebrews explains in detail).

Because of this relationship, it is clear that Christ fulfilled Judaism; but it does not follow at all that Christ fulfils other religions. If in any sense Christ fulfils other religions, that must be shown by an entirely different argument.

Truth

From what has just been said, it may appear that Christian belief consists of faith in certain doctrines or statements. It is right to distinguish between faith in God or in Christ, and faith in a statement or proposition. True Christian faith is indeed faith in God and in Christ. But it does not follow that faith in doctrines is excluded. It is not a matter of either/or, but both/ and. It is possible to believe in a set of doctrines without having any faith in God himself. But the reverse is not the case. For to believe in God is to believe in a certain sort of God; in other words, faith in God involves belief in certain things about him. Certainly it will include (for example) a feeling of dependence; but also some intellectual ideas. Even a feeling of dependence involves a belief that God is such that one can depend on him.

What we are saying, then, is that Christian faith involves belief that certain statements are true. Now this is questioned by some, as it is claimed that religious language does not make statements of facts, but rather reveals attitudes or intentions.

Thus some claim that the statement, 'I believe in God', really means, 'I intend to act in such a way'. All we need say here is that such reductionist interpretation depends on a positivistic philosophy, which we do not find it necessary to accept. Indeed, a statement of belief in God ought to include an intention to live in a certain way; but the statement cannot be reduced to that intention. In ordinary speech, and certainly here, we are saying that certain statements are factually true.

We must consider the consequences of this; for if certain statements are true, then certain other statements are not true. Thus if we claim that certain statements made in the Christian faith are true, we shall be asserting implicitly that certain statements made in other religions are not true. It may well be that some statements owe their form to the particular culture in which they arise, and it may well be that some of the conflict of ideas in different religions can be overcome by recognising the cultural differences. Thus Christianity may be put into different thought-forms to make it intelligible in different parts of the world. But although this may remove some difficulties, it does not remove the 'scandal of particularity' of Jesus Christ himself. Christ is not just an incarnate deity anywhere, but he is Jesus Christ, God incarnate in Jesus of Nazareth in the first century A.D., in Palestine.

So the Christian belief in God as Trinity associates God with Christianity in particular, and thereby makes a claim not only to be true, but to be the unique truth, which is incompatible with certain other truth-claims.

Such a claim may immediately call forth the accusation of conceit and intolerance. There is indeed the danger of conceit, but the Christian, in making his claim to have the truth, is claiming that it has been revealed; and he is claiming to have only what he has been given. Indeed, the attitude is not one of conceit, but of humility, in bowing to the Lordship of Christ. The claim to truth is a part of the acceptance of Jesus Christ as Lord.

The charge of intolerance makes the assumption that intolerance is an evil thing. We must not assume that without question. Intolerance of people is an evil thing; we do not try to suppress people. But if a teacher of mathematics gets a wrong answer from his pupil, he will not accept it, but will be intolerant of the false answer. Truth is intolerant.

Again we must be careful not to make too big assumptions. If we start from a Christian basis, we may feel compelled to make certain affirmations concerning what is true; but that does not enable us to make categorical statements about all non-Christian beliefs. In other words, if Christianity is true, it does not follow that everything in every other religion is false. If, as Christians certainly believe, God created the world and everything in it, then it is not impossible that some may recognize some of his handiwork. Moreover, if God made man in his own image, man at least has the capacity to know God, and there may be a vestigial knowledge of God in man. Of course, Christians believe not only in God's creation, but also in man's fall; and therefore man's capacity to recognize God's handiwork and to know God is seriously impaired. Perhaps man cannot know God at all unaided; but if man can know God through his special revelation in Christ, perhaps he can also know him through his general revelation in nature and by his image in man. We may speak of God's special grace in Christ, and of his common grace given to those not yet in Christ, grace which prevents man going to utter corruption, and may even lead him to God.

There are cases recorded where those who have proclaimed the Christian faith in certain areas for the first time have had an immediate response, and it appears that the previous beliefs of the people were a preparation for receiving the Christian Gospel. In some such cases those who have heard and accepted the Gospel have asked why the messengers did not come before. Two possible deductions may be made from this. First, there may be some knowledge of the true God outside Christianity; secondly, such knowledge, if it exists, is inadequate. It is possible that while we have the light of the knowledge of the glory of God in the face of Jesus Christ (2 Cor. 4:6), in full brilliance, there may be a dim flicker available still outside of Christ. But it must be added that this is speculation, and that the cases of immediate response, just mentioned, are not the normal experience.

The question now arises about the destiny of those outside the Christian faith. If we are seeking a theological basis for our consideration, we have to be careful. If Scripture makes no direct, categorical statements, then we cannot do so either. If we make deductions from general principles as revealed in Scripture, then we have to remember that these have only the secondary value of deductions, and no more. They may be false deductions. Thus it is a dangerous argument to say (with John Hick) that God would not condemn millions to hell. How does he know that? This is a deduction based solely on his view of God's love, and does not appear to take into account God's righteousness and human responsibility (Rom. 3:19). We must add two further comments: we know the outworkings of God's love and righteousness only as far as he has revealed them; and finally God himself is Judge: we are not.

What is clear from Scripture is that those who accept Christ have eternal life; those who reject him do not. But what of those who have never heard? There is only the slightest hint of an answer in Scripture, in Rom. 1:18–20 and 2:15–16, and also in Rom. 2:7. Possibly any who trust God and seek to serve him as far as they know him, will be accepted as Abraham, being justified by faith. In such a case, salvation would be by Christ alone, even though Christ were not known. It must be stressed that any such deduction is pure speculation. The Scriptures reveal information not for our curiosity, but for our obedience; therefore the Scriptural answer must be, Go and tell them.

We have tried to see so far what the Christian message really is, in outline, and the unique claims that Christianity makes for itself. The next matter for consideration is how Christianity can be communicated to non-Christians.

Problems in Dialogue

A fashionable word today is 'dialogue'; but fashion is no reason for either accepting or rejecting it. When two parties are in dispute, negotiations are begun from two different positions, with the hope that, after some concessions from each side, a 'formula' will be agreed on by both sides. Certain observations may be made. First, the formula is not infrequently a form of words which can be interpreted in different ways by the two sides, so that the dispute may end without loss of face by either side, and without necessarily reaching actual agreement. Now some people do use the term 'dialogue' in this sense, and they try to find a common core of religion, a sort of agreed formula, throughout the world. They have not yet succeeded, but this is their aim.

However, if we are considering a theological basis for dialogue, it will be clear from the first part of this chapter that the Christian will be a rather intransigent partner in dialogue. He is not in a position to negotiate and to make concessions. He starts from the position that Christianity is revealed truth and that Christ is the final revelation of God, and he cannot be superseded. He is not entering into dialogue to find the truth, but he has already found the truth, though that claim does not imply that he has or knows all the truth. But at the very least he has found the basic truth. His fundamental position is one of having found, rather than of still seeking.

Some would say that what the Christian asserts is by faith rather than by knowledge. Perhaps this is restricting the term 'knowledge' too much. If we claim to know only what we have fully proved and demonstrated to be the case, then perhaps the only real knowledge is mathematical knowledge. But we normally say that we *know* when we feel that the evidence is sufficiently strong and when it is psychologically convincing. A Christian, accepting the Lordship of Christ, takes up his position by faith. But as a result of that faith he does claim to know, and not just to imagine or think. His knowledge is an interpretation of the evidence, by faith. And put thus, it may be seen that Christian knowledge is not so far different from other forms of knowledge.

Once the Christian has acknowledged the Lordship of Christ, or, in other words, has entered the Kingdom of God, he finds that he is not completely open to dialogue, in that his own position is not negotiable. Accepting Jesus Christ as Lord is not just a working hypothesis which may be altered in the course of negotiation. Far otherwise. It is a self-commitment to obedience to him. It is not merely an idea, but an attitude of one's whole being. This is the theological basis on which a Christian enters dialogue. Loyalty to Christ limits dialogue.

The Christian feels a further limit to dialogue in that the natural man's mind is blinded by sin, so that rational argument alone is not sufficient. In this respect the parables are of interest, because they do not so much give new information for consideration, but present a new way of looking at things, a new insight, or a new perspective.

If God has indeed spoken, then it is more appropriate for his Word to judge men, than for men to judge his Word. Proclamation of his Word would seem to be more suitable than discussion of it. Many passages in the Bible which at first sight appear to be cases of dialogue turn out, on further examination, to be otherwise. Thus a question may be posed not in order to get a reply, but rather to evoke thought. A rhetorical question is a powerful way of making a statement, in that it both raises a question and at the same time implicitly provides the answer. 'Who would think that?' is a dramatic way of saying, 'No-one would think that.'

Possibilities in Dialogue

With these warnings about the limits of dialogue which has a Christian theological basis, we may now proceed to consider its possibilities. If we consider solely revealed truth, we shall be inclined towards declaration or proclamation, rather than dialogue. But if we consider God's grace and its manifestations, we shall see the appropriateness of dialogue. God is under no form of constraint or obligation to come to man's aid; indeed God could in all righteousness exterminate man for his sins. But in his infinite grace God has provided salvation for man, and because man has fallen so far from God, God's grace has extended to the very depths into which man has fallen. So the grace of God is adequate to meet the need of man. God sent his prophets to men just where they were. But the desperate nature of man's plight was such that he was not only lost, but also ignorant of the fact, and of himself not desirous of receiving God's salvation.

Jeremiah is a conspicuous example of a messenger of God enacting God's grace. Jeremiah did not only proclaim 'Thus saith the Lord', but he also made his personal plea to the people to turn to God. He was evidently at heart one with both God and the people. It was as one of the people that he pleaded with them.

The most conspicuous example of all is the Incarnation. Here God did not merely proclaim to men, but entered into humanity and spoke as man to man. The Lord Jesus Christ was utterly loyal to God, and at the same time entered human life and spoke the language of men as they understood it. He spoke not only as God, but also as man.

Communication is not the same as proclamation; it is quite possible to proclaim a message which is not understood. In this case there is no communication, and the message, despite being proclaimed, is not passed on to the hearers. In order to communicate, the speaker must achieve understanding in his hearers. A child may understand every single word which the teacher has used, but, because the concepts are beyond his experience, he may not understand anything. The teacher therefore must see the way the child thinks, and use the thought-forms, as well as the words, which the child uses.

This is the nature of true dialogue. The speaker sees the questions which are in the mind of the hearer, and addresses himself to them. This may be a long process, but the good teacher soon learns that there is a limit to the speed with which he can communicate new ideas to his pupils. The question and answer method is common with teachers. The teacher does not (usually) ask questions because he wants to know; he already knows; but it is to provoke thought and to lead the pupil to the answer. The teacher both asks questions himself and also encourages the pupil to ask questions. This is the use of dialogue in communicating the understanding of information. There is (normally) no idea of negotiating, and the teacher is not aiming at an agreement in which both sides make some concessions. Rather he is aiming at communicating information about facts which he already knows.

Such dialogue is concerned not only with the importance of the message, but also with the importance of the person who is to receive it. It is a case of treating the person genuinely as a person, and not as a thing. It is the way of love. Moreover it is the way of confidence. The timid teacher presents the material and does not allow questions, for fear of being caught out and unable to answer. The teacher who is the master of his material is not afraid to be questioned, and if, on the odd occasion, he does not know the answer, he is not afraid to say so, and then to try to find out. So it is with communicating the Gospel. One who has confidence can enter into dialogue, as he knows where he stands.

The Presentation of the Christian Message in the New Testament

The language of Jesus, and in particular the parables, exemplify the principles which we have been examining. The parables are not just illustrations; they are ways of entering into the world of the hearers, and arousing such feelings as surprise, shock, concern, anger; there is an emotional, as well as an intellectual, reaction. Thus with the parable of the labourers in the vineyard, first Jesus enters into the everyday world of his hearers with an everyday sort of story, but then the story has a surprising twist, and the hearers are surprised at God's grace. It is something unexpected. So with other parables, there is the usual, which gains sympathy, and the unusual, which produces surprise. It was the Tax-man, rather than the Pharisee, whose prayer was answered; the Samaritan, rather than the Priest or Levite, who was commended for being a good neighbour.

In the beatitudes there is the same element of surprise, but without the supporting parable. Those who are counted blessed in the Kingdom of God are those who are perhaps considered unfortunate in the world. Worldly values are faced – and reversed. Here is a way of confronting men with what interests them, their own values and standards, and then presenting the Gospel in the light of this, and indeed as its opposite. There is dialogue in the sense of meeting the hearers on their own ground, and facing their questions; but there is no suggestion of negotiating a compromise.

The early Christian preaching was suited to its audiences. Thus in addressing Jews (Acts 2:14–36), Peter explained about Jesus Christ in terms of Jewish hopes and expectations. In speaking to unsophisticated pagans (Acts 14:14–18), Paul could only go as far as talking about nature and God as its Creator. But to sophisticated pagans in Athens (Acts 17:22–34), he referred to their city, their altar, their poets and their philosophy. However, he proceeded from what was acceptable to what caused offence, namely, mention of Jesus and the resurrection.

It is notable that Paul's method was not just to proclaim, but also to argue, explain, prove, proclaim and persuade (Acts 17:1–4). He entered into dialogue, not to make any concessions, but to answer questions and to produce understanding.

Clearly then there is a place for human reasoning. In the New Testament, faith is opposed to sight, and not to reason. In his dealing with the Corinthians (as shown in 1 Corinthians), Paul argued his case, and did not simply give authoritative answers. He faced their questions.

Silence or Speech?

Words can vary in their sense and can lose their meaning. Thus a 'standard' car used to be one which was up to standard, that is, good. But as de luxe and super-de luxe models arrive, 'standard' finds itself at the bottom of the list, instead of the top. In the same way Christian words can lose their value, sometimes because nominal Christians have destroyed the true meaning. As a result of this, some advocate 'Christian presence', suggesting that Christians have no right to speak, because of past failures.

In exceptional circumstances it may be that a silent Christian presence is all that is possible, as 'actions speak louder than words'. But that is not the normal Christian pattern. Words and actions go together. Jesus' action in washing the disciples' feet showed what he meant by humility, and his eating with sinners illustrated his view of God's grace. Christians should indeed have a Christian presence, and their lives should illustrate the Gospel; but normally that is no substitute for stating the Gospel in words. Social action is an outcome of the Gospel, but not a substitute for it, nor a total expression of it.

In dialogue there is the danger of the misuse of words. As we have already pointed out, 'Christianity' has many meanings today. We are concerned to keep to its original and apostolic meaning. 'God' can also have various meanings; in Christianity the term refers to God as Trinity; not just the Absolute, but the God of Abraham. 'Christ' is not just a cosmic Being, but the Lord Jesus Christ in particular. To use these words in vague and generalized senses may produce a 'formula' of agreement, but that is not the purpose of Christian dialogue.

Current Ways of Thinking

There are certain fashions in thought. One at the moment is phenomenology. It claims to look at appearances without *a priori* theological judgments, and to see from the evidence whether thére is one common core of religious experience manifest in all religions. It assumes (as Troeltsch did at the beginning of this century) that the study of history is objective, while the study of theology is subjective. This itself is a subjective judgment. Such a notional objectivity is really bogus. It is just the substitution of one set of presuppositions for another. Thus Hick, in a historical survey of various religions in the world about a thousand years before Christ, refers to sudden changes which he calls 'revelatory moments'. Far from being objective, this is a distinct judgment on the significance of these events.

Another fashion is existentialism. This stresses what is true *for me*. It has a value in calling attention to the practical effect of religious belief, but it also has a danger in obscuring the whole issue of truth. We are concerned not merely with what is true for me, subjectively, but with what is true, objectively, whether I care to believe it or not.

'Historical consciousness' is also in fashion. It is somewhat similar to the theory of stimulus and response in behaviouristic psychology. There is such a thing as stimulus and response, but it does not explain everything. So in historical study we may see various movements and ideas as affected by situations; but that does not mean that the whole concept of truth and error can be lost in a series of reactions. Reaction may be one factor; but truth and orthodoxy are still valid concepts.

These fashions of modern thought may employ dialogue in a way which we find less than adequate. But we do not therefore have to abandon dialogue. Rather we have to use it in a way which is consistent with our Christian theological position. With that basis we can confidently engage in dialogue. In gaining further insights from other ways of thinking, we are careful not to abandon or neglect the evangelical insights which we already have. Above all, we are bound by our loyalty to Christ himself as Lord, and Christ as witnessed to in the New Testament.

5

Non-Christian Religions: Some Biblical Guidelines

KENNETH G. HOWKINS

AS WE ATTEMPT TO FORMULATE A CHRISTIAN APPROACH TO non-Christian religions and their adherents, we are bound to ask whether the Bible gives any detailed guidance. Some people seem to assume that no such guidance is available, but we have already seen in Chapter Three and on pages 00–00 that it is possible to learn both from what we are told about Jesus Christ and from the early Christian preaching. In point of fact, the Bible contains a good deal of material that is relevant.

The Preaching of Paul

Paul, the Apostle to the Gentiles, gives us an example which is worthy of some consideration. When he spoke to Jews, his approach was like that of Peter at Pentecost. After all, he *was* a Jew, and understood as much as any man could of how Jews thought, felt and acted, of their hopes and aspirations. His own experience was first that of a Jew who rejected the Lord Jesus Christ with all his heart, and then that of a Jew who accepted him with all his heart. He was therefore ideally qualified to present Christ to Jews. In essence, he tried to show them that Jesus of Nazareth was the One for whom their nation had been looking for centuries, the One who had not been recognised at first; but now, because of his resurrection, it was clear that he was the promised Messiah, put to death by men but raised and highly exalted by God. The basis of this argument was Scripture (that is, of course, the Old Testament) and witness to the resurrection.

In principle this was quite simple. Paul and his audience shared a common background, which was in fact the background of Christianity itself. The task was just to present Jesus as the fulfilment of Judaism. Of course, the message was not always received in such a simple and logical fashion, but further discussion and argument followed the same line of thought. A detailed example of this approach is given in Acts 13:13–44.

It may be noted that the audience included some Gentiles as well as Jews. These are called 'God-fearers', that is, those who had come to admire the Jewish religion and follow it as far as they could without actually becoming full converts or proselytes, and without submitting to the ritual obligations of the Law. Because their outlook was so similar to that of Jews, Paul could preach to them with the Jews. There were no special problems. Indeed it was the reverse: for the God-fearers, Christianity was a short cut to acceptance with God, without all the burden of the Law (as Paul argued cogently in his letter to the Galatians).

When Paul met some unsophisticated Gentiles at Lystra (Acts 14:8–18), and they began to treat him and his companion as gods, he had to act in some haste. He did not give a formal discourse or enter into dialogue with them; but perhaps his instant, off-the-cuff plea to them revealed an approach which he had already thought out. He appealed to the common humanity which he shared with them (v. 15) and to what we may call 'creation theology' (vv. 15–17). He did not preach the Gospel, because it would have been quite unintelligible to them. But, as in addressing Jews, he used the common ground, though this covered a very limited area. This common ground was both within their experience and understanding, and was also the basis on which in due time and with due preparation the Gospel could be presented. We shall investigate this in more detail later.

Paul at Athens

At Athens Paul faced a quite different crowd of Gentiles (Acts

17:16–34). Possibly he had intended to keep quiet until his friends arrived, but the sight of the city 'full of idols' so provoked him that he could not keep quiet. In the synagogue he argued with Jews and God-fearers, and in the market place with anyone who happened to be there. As a result he was called upon to explain himself before a sophisticated audience. Paul was quite equal to the occasion, as his background was not only Jewish: he had been brought up in Tarsus in Cilicia, a centre of Stoic philosophy, and his education included all the benefits of both Jewish and Gentile learning.

Again, Paul finds what he has in common with his audience, draws attention to this, and goes on further. He comments that they are very religious. That may be said with approval; but he did not approve of the nature of their religion; yet he did not immediately say so. First he elaborated on what he found there which was acceptable. What they worshipped as unknown, he was making known. He spoke in terms of creation theology again. He added that God did not dwell in man-made shrines, echoing not only the Old Testament, but also the Greek Euripides. Following his creation theology along the line of divine providence, he echoed sentiments agreeable to the Epicurean philosophers (that God, being self-sufficient, did not need men's gifts) and to the Stoic philosophers (that God is the source of all life). In talking next of the unity of the human race as created by God, he was alluding to the biblical creation stories and also agreeing with what was implicit in Stoicism, but gently rebuking the proud claim of the Athenians to superiority. Next Paul quotes from Greek poets, Epimenides, Aratus and Cleanthes, not giving total approval to all that they say, but quoting certain lines which were in fact part of both Greek and Christian thought, and making deductions from them. The main deductions are that God is such that, first, it is possible to find him, and, secondly, he is not like any image. Once Paul had demonstrated, evidently without disapproval, something of the nature of God himself, he was able to go on to state something of Christianity itself. The appeal is not philosophical, but moral. He speaks of righteousness, repentance and judgment. Still there is no opposition. But when he mentions the resurrection of Christ as that which gives certainty of the facts just mentioned, he receives a mixture of mockery and interest. The point which was really unacceptable to Greek thought was the Resurrection. Paul was no doubt aware of this.

Paul's Missionary Principles

Certain observations may be made here. Paul's motivation in speaking in the first place was that he just had to. He could not help it! As a result of the interest aroused, he was called on to give a formal explanation, and used the opportunity to the full. His method was not to launch immediately into a condemnation of the false religion which had aroused him, but to find points of contact and of approval. The theology which underlies his approach is basically that of Creation and the Wisdom Literature of the Old Testament. However, his direct references and quotations are associated not with the Old Testament, but with Greek thought and literature. Thus Paul shows himself flexible in his method, but uncompromising in his message. The amount which Paul said about Christianity on this occasion was limited, the immediate reason being apparently that his hearers had had enough at that point; but it may well be that Paul in fact said as much as he thought appropriate for that occasion.

The Bible and Other Religions

We should expect that Paul's attitude to people of other religions would be similar to that expressed in the Old Testament. To this we must now turn. In general, in the Old Testament other religions are regarded as a threat to Israel's own faith. God had revealed Himself to Abraham and his successors, to Moses, and to the prophets. There was the constant struggle to remain faithful to the Lord, in the face of other religions, which, for various reasons, seemed to be attractive. There was no consideration, either practical or academic, of any relationship between the true religion of Israel and other religions. Where there is the loftiest picture of the God of Israel, he is portrayed as the only God, and other religions are simply false. But this one God is the God of the whole world, and all peoples are invited to share in his salvation (see the second part of the Book of Isaiah in particular).

In the New Testament the same attitude continues, as the fulness of the revelation and salvation of God are given in Christ. Thus it is boldly stated that there is salvation in no other name (Acts 4:12). Nevertheless, there are slight hints that those who have no direct knowledge of God or of Christ, but have faith in God as far as they know him, are accepted (Rom. 2:7–11). Also, the New Testament, looking back (Rom. 10:14–21), seems to imply that God could be known outside Israel.

There is no clear reference in the Bible to a genuine response to God being made in other religions, but there are references to non-Israelites accepting Israel's God, and being accepted by him, for example, Rahab, Naaman, the widow of Zarephath and the Ninevites. When Peter spoke to Cornelius, a Roman who had come to accept Israel's God in all sincerity, he (Peter) said, 'God does not have favourites; but anybody of any nationality who fears God and does what is right is acceptable to him' (Acts 10:34). The double condition here is to be noted: fear God and do what is right.

The only apparent reference in the Bible to genuine worship of the true God taking place in other religions, outside the Judaeo-Christian revelation, is Malachi 1:11; but this is of uncertain interpretation.

Creation Theology

Now we shall look at the theology underlying Paul's approach to those of other religions. As has been stated already, he did not quote from the Old Testament, but his thought was moulded and guided by it. A very large part of the Old Testament deals with the special revelation of God to the patriarchs and prophets, leading on to the coming of Christ. To non-Israelites who were not familiar with this revelation, references to the Old Testament would be meaningless. But if we go back further, to the times before the call of Abraham and before the Exodus, we reach what is of universal relevance. The call of Abraham was for one man; the Exodus of the Israelites was for one nation; but Creation and its theology are significant for all mankind. It is worthy of notice that the prophets (especially Isaiah 40ff.) were concerned to bring Israel back not just to the Sinaitic Covenant, but to creation theology, relating God's sovereignty to all nations.

Thus Genesis 1–11 is basic to the biblical outlook. There are various new beginnings throughout the Bible: with Abraham, the Exodus, the Exile and Christ there were new beginnings; but at Creation there was the beginning of the earth and of the whole human race.

The fact of Creation means that the world and man do not have their origins and explanation within themselves, but outside themselves. They are contingent. The fact that all was created, and did not just happen, implies purpose: the purpose of the Creator in his creation is reflected in man's purposiveness. To have purposes is part of being human.

The facts of creation and purpose lead on to the reality of history. History is neither mechanistic, in the sense that everything happens by a mechanical cause and effect; nor is it cyclical, in the sense that it just repeats itself. Rather, there are real possibilities and real choices; and when actions take place, what is past influences the future, but does not determine it. New actions ever make new possibilities. The total freedom of God's initial and continued action produces a limited freedom for man's actions. Thus our understanding of history follows from our understanding of creation.

Creation and Man

The doctrine of Creation reveals certain things about the nature of man. Ideally man has a relationship with God, with his fellow men, and with nature. But the biblical picture shows Creation as being declared good by the Creator, but then marred by man's disobedience to his Creator. Thus man has lost his fellowship with God; the unity of mankind is marred by disharmony between men and the joy of procreating is accompanied by the pains of childbirth; sorrow and hardship are involved in man's task of subduing the earth. The story of the Tower of Babel shows further man's rebellion against God, and the consequent scattered disorder and mutual incomprehension among men.

At all levels, man suffers the baleful effects of his fall. With his broken relationship with God, human, false religions arise. With the broken relationships between men, racial disharmony, conflict and war arise. And as man makes his tools to subdue the earth, so also he makes weapons of destruction. Thus it is characteristic of mankind, created in the image of God, but fallen, that all his culture is both good in that it is an expression of his activity as made in God's image, but tainted, in that he is fallen. It is neither wholly good nor wholly bad.

If this line of thought is pursued, then it is to be expected that men's religions will contain something of good but also something which is not good. It must be remembered also that God is immanent as well as transcendent; that God has not entirely ceased his gracious activity among men; there is the 'common grace' of God operating in the world, preventing it from becoming entirely corrupt, as well as the special grace of God, operating in and through Christ and by his Holy Spirit. Perhaps also 'the true light that enlightens every man' (John 1:9), which came into the world in fulness in the incarnation, also gives some illumination to all. If all of this is so, then it explains how Paul can find some points of contact in the religion of the Athenians: it is not absolutely and completely false. This also explains how Paul can envisage the possibility of some men's responding to God and being accepted by him, even when they have not directly received God's special revelation as given through the prophets and the Son.

Consideration along these lines will make us realise more of the greatness of God: he is not really totally dependent on us for communicating his grace to men. Perhaps he has worked among the 'heathen' before Christians have arrived with the Good News. These considerations have arisen from the doctrine of Creation.

The story of the Flood, also in the early chapters of Genesis, is closely linked with Creation. A new start was made, and in the story of Noah there are various direct allusions to the Creation story: the cosmic covenant with Noah accords with Creation theology; there is reaffirmation of man being in God's image and man's role to have dominion (Gen. 1:26–31 and 9:6–7); the natural laws made by God (Gen. 1:9–13 and 8:22); man's sin and guilt (Gen. 3:1–24 and 6:1–8); God's mercy and grace (Gen. 3:15 and 8:22). It is not said that all will be saved, but that all will have the chance of repentance.

The Wisdom Literature

The Wisdom Literature of the Old Testament (Proverbs, Ecclesiastes and Job) is an important part of the Bible, to which inadequate attention is often given. Sometimes it is viewed as basically ethical rather than religious in its outlook, and the assumption is made that the religious elements were added afterwards. But this is a radical misunderstanding. The religion is fundamental. In fact, the Wisdom Literature is set within the framework of Creation theology, and it has a universal outlook. It is not tied specifically to the revelation of God and his salvation made to the patriarchs and prophets, but to God as Creator, and to the practical obligations which come to man in recognizing him. Peter's words, already quoted above, that anybody 'who fears God and does what is right' (Acts 10:34) is acceptable to God, are in complete accord with the Wisdom Literature.

As this literature does not presuppose knowledge of God through the Judaeo-Christian revelation, but is based on the most fundamental Creation theology, it may well be that this is the best bridge between biblical religion as culminating in Christianity and non-Christian religions, as was suggested by D. A. Hubbard, in the Tyndale Bulletin of 1966. He refers in particular to those religions which have no sense of history, and adds, 'By emphasizing the fear of the Lord and the faithful discharge of one's duty ... wisdom literature points the way by which a world bogged down in meaninglessness can find some firm ground of purpose'.

The book of Proverbs deals with the ordinary obligations of daily living; Ecclesiastes traces the various attempts made to find some meaning and purpose in life, all of which end in a feeling of futility and frustration, until the final advice is given to 'remember thy Creator in the days of thy youth'; and Job grapples desperately with the problem of suffering, finding the practical answer in simple acceptance of God in all his greatness. The substance of these books, then, may well make a direct appeal to the life and experiences of men who are not impressed with Christianity in its fulness. This may well be a valuable way in. We may add that sophisticated 'pagans' in some of our school sixth forms, when making a study of Ecclesiastes, have exclaimed, 'He is asking just the sort of questions that we ask!'

The suggestion is not that the Wisdom Literature is all that we give, instead of Christianity, but that this may be the point of contact, the starting point. It is perhaps relevant to remember that the Wisdom Literature of the Old Testament has some direct literary connections with the Wisdom Literature of the surrounding nations. While the religions were different, the practical experiences of everyday life were similar, and hence there could be some interchange at this level. But within the Old Testament this literature is intimately allied with the fear of the Lord. In a similar way, the contact with those of other religions may start on the non-religious level of the practical problems of living. If God is indeed the Creator, then these everyday experiences are within his creation, a creation which bears his stamp. Thus (according to Eph. 3:14–15) all earthly fatherhood is known from God the Father; so that in the human experience of the father-son relationship there is some reflection of the divine Fatherhood.

Non-Christian religions, and in particular such as are found in India, employ an entirely different mode of thought from that in Christianity. For this reason, making a contact or bridge is difficult, and the idea of Christianity as 'fulfilling' these religions is just not valid for those who have these religions. It is no use scratching somebody where it does not itch! A pedagogy of the spread of Christianity to those of other religions must follow the educational principle of being 'child-centred', that is, keeping in mind the experience, vocabulary, concepts and understanding of those being taught, whether they are children or adults. Therefore the religious concepts of Christianity may be the wrong starting point: they must be preceded by ordinary, everyday experience. Thus the ideas within the Wisdom Literature of the Old Testament, and Creation Theology with its implications, are points of contact. But again it must be stressed that this is not a substitute for the Gospel, but a preparation for it. The good teacher has to order his syllabus, and knows that he cannot hurry through it, skipping the earlier parts, which are foundational.

It is relevant here to refer again to the parables of Jesus. He, the great Teacher, in communicating spiritual truths began with parables which dealt with the ordinary experiences of everyday life.

Recent Approaches

So far we have tried to see something of the Christian approach to those of other religions as exemplified in Paul, and as implicit or explicit in the rest of Scripture. Now we shall look at the practical situation as seen in the last two centuries or so, and up to the present time.

The attitude of Christians to other religions depends on their own understanding of Christianity and on their understanding of the other religions in question, and all is affected, to at any rate some extent, by the general intellectual and religious climate of the times. In both spheres, this understanding has changed considerably in the last hundred years. Moreover, it has to be remembered that there are many different understandings of Christianity by Christians, and similarly many different understandings of other religions by their adherents. Hence it is not possible simply to set out *the* approach of Christians to, say, Hinduism.

Until comparatively recent times, Christians have been too concerned with their own beliefs to make objective estimates of their attitudes towards other religions. In fact, other religions were considered either as entirely false, and of the devil, or as containing some measure of truth which could be a bridge to Christianity. (Such attitudes were seen in the early days of the church, the former being exemplified by Justin Martyr and Tertullian, and the latter by Clement of Alexandria.) These religions were not studied in their own right.

But changes have been taking place over the last two centuries, with the result that many in the 'Christian' world have begun to have a lower view of Christianity than previously, and a higher view of other religions. There has been available an increasing amount of knowledge about other religions, ancient and modern, and with the theory of evolution applied to everything human – man's body, mind, institutions and religions – religion became, for some, a subject emptied of personal experience and subjected to cold description, analysis and explanation. For such 'rationalists' (as they fondly claim to be) all religions were just 'there', and all were equally true or false.

Many factors have been involved in these changes. The sacred writings of other world religions became available in translation, thus showing more favourable aspects of these religions. Moreover some of these religions began to reform themselves as a result of the impact of western culture. Some of the major religions, such as Hinduism, Buddhism and Islam, have acquired a new vitality, and this has been associated with a new nationalism. It has led to a new sense of mission.

Many westerners have shown a sense of guilt, as a reaction against former colonialism, and many feel disillusioned with organized religion. A further reaction against colonialism is the special sympathy which is felt for minorities. Following from these feelings is the tendency to condemn spreading Christianity as 'indoctrination', in a pejorative sense. Then there is a popular relativism, which exalts toleration as the supreme virtue and rejects exclusive claims to truth. This mode of thinking is characteristic of Hinduism, but is often accepted uncritically in the west as being self-evident.

For many, Christianity has undergone various changes and modifications as a result of the growth and impact of science. Thus the Resurrection, in its full sense, is ignored or denied in many quarters, and so what remains is an emasculated Christianity, with its truth-claims invalidated. Hence there has been the tendency to assume that all past Christian attitudes to other religions have been wrong.

The new Christian answer to all these changes came in the form of the idea of 'fulfilment'. As Christianity fulfilled Judaism, so, the claim went, it fulfilled Hinduism, meeting its deepest needs and longings. A brief critique of this is bound to be somewhat simplistic. But in essence, the virtue of the method is that it involved genuine sympathy, and care to try to understand Hinduism accurately. However its vice is that it fails to do justice to either Christianity or Hinduism: it in fact employed a liberalized form of Christianity with Christ as uniquely God-conscious, rather than uniquely God's Son; and it answered 'Hindu' questions which Hindus did not ask.

In the realm of theology, Liberal Protestantism found a redoubtable opponent in Karl Barth, whose approach became known as Dialectical Theology and Neo-orthodoxy. He stressed the sovereignty and transcendence of God, condemning all things human, including even Christianity as a religion ('religion' being a human invention) and Christian apologetics. Everything depended on God, who could be known not by argument, but only by encounter – on God's initiative.

Hendrik Kraemer took this line of thought into Christian missionary strategy. He insisted that the task was not to make the Gospel acceptable, but to make it inescapable. He wrote (in 1938) that there was no continuity between the Christian Gospel and non-Christian religions, the former being of God, the latter of man; that God is the God of creation, of redemption and of history. He considered that although God was at work in the world, man, because of his own corruption, could not discern this. Thus there was no point of contact between Christianity and other religions, because, if God was working in other religions, sinful man could not recognise this work.

The tendency now is to stress the immanence rather than the transcendence of God, that is, his working in the world rather than his lofty and glorious exaltation above it. This tendency naturally has a large effect on present considerations of the relationship between Christianity and other religions. But we do not need to follow such tendencies: rather, we need to keep in mind the Scriptural balance of both the transcendence and the immanence of God. If either one of these is more relevant in any particular discussion, we still need to be careful that the conclusion does not deny the other. Again we may recall that Creation Theology does keep the transcendence and immanence of God together in balance, showing him as being distinct and separate from his creation, and high above it, yet at the same time active in it.

At the present time there is two-way traffic: not only is Christianity trying to gain more ground in the East, but also Eastern religions are increasingly coming to the West, in various forms. Elsewhere the major world religions are facing each other without the influence of colonialism.

Present Approaches

There is now a widespread dissatisfaction with past solutions to questions of the relations of Christianity with other religions, and a desire for new solutions. The tendency is to look, not for what is common to all religions, the lowest common denominator, but for what is common to all men, their common humanity. The Hindu, Buddhist, Muslim and Christian each has his religion, and there are great differences. But each is also a man, and in this they are all the same. So the approach is not to a man's religion, but to the man himself. The Christian sees this humanity as created by God himself (and, as a Christian, he will want to add, through Christ, with redemption achieved by Christ and spiritual awakening possible by the Holy Spirit). The Christian, then, has this humanity in common with all men. A Christian attitude of sympathy towards those of other faiths will not show condescension, but that humility which characterized the Christian's Lord, who came not to be served, but to serve (Mark 10:45), in a way that led even to death.

In the first place, giving respect to a person as a person includes giving respect to his religious convictions. This entails neither accepting nor rejecting the religion itself, but accepting the sincerity of the person. If there is mutual sincerity, both given and accepted, then a relationship can be established. This can lead to understanding, and on to dialogue. When the Christian enters into dialogue with the non-Christian, the religious views of the two may have little or nothing in common. But what the two persons do have in common is their humanity and their human experiences of life. This is the starting point, and links with what we have said about the Wisdom Literature of the Old Testament. Dialogue involves going on from this point, to have a genuine interchange of ideas; and communication (as distinct from proclamation) involves not just stating ideas, but getting them over so that they are understood. It should be added that 'understood' does not necessarily imply 'accepted'. Our task as Christians is to help others to understand something of Christianity, and whether they accept it or not is the task of the Holy Spirit of God.

Religions which are basically man-centred can happily co-exist. Thus classical Hinduism, which is primarily a philosophical anthropology and only secondarily and in-directly possesses a theology, accepts all religions as valid ways to the ultimate goal. But Christianity (of the biblical sort) is fundamentally God-centred and Christ-centred, and cannot accept other religions as entirely valid without denying itself. For this reason the Christian, in contemplating an approach to other religions, has to decide whether to start from full-scale, biblical, God-centred, Christ-centred Christianity, and pro-ceed to a head-on collision; or whether to start with the neutral ground of our common humanity and build up from there. It is not a question of the final content of the Christian message, but of the way, and the order, in which it is presented.

There are eviscerated forms of Christianity (such as Til-lich's) which aim ultimately at self-understanding and grasp-ing the meaning of existence. Such forms will provoke no clash with other religions, because they have removed 'the scandal of particularity' and every cause of clashing. In fact, Tillich-type Christianity would not clash with Hinduism, for the sim-ple reason that it has already, in effect, changed itself into Hinduism. This sort of Christianity does not clash with other religions, but it does clash with biblical Christianity.

The Task

The distinctive Christian message is the living Christ, and all doctrinal formulations are quite secondary. The aim of Christ-ian proclamation is that the hearer should have an encounter with the living Christ, crucified and raised from the dead. Herein lies the answer to questions of guilt and forgiveness, wholeness, and meaning in life. Doctrines alone are dead; but the risen Christ both has life and gives life. Doctrines are not, however, irrelevant; for if 'Christ' is presented with false or inadequate doctrine, then this is not the true Christ.

The starting point of communicating the Good News may well be our common humanity; but the finishing point is Christ's unique deity. Without that starting point there may be no communication; without that finishing point there will be no Good News. Between the starting and finishing points

72

there needs to be a careful, sympathetic and accurate under-standing of those to whom we wish to communicate, in order to understand how and why they think and feel as they do. Also there needs to be a careful and accurate understanding of Christianity itself, in order to see what is fundamental and essential, and what is solely its cultural accretion in our west-ern world of the twentieth century. Neither task is easy; each is vital. But this is not the end: the task, after removing the non-essential outer-garments of our culture from the Gospel, is to reclothe it in the language and thought-forms of those to whom we present it. Perhaps it is this task which makes genuine dialogue an essential prerequisite of proclamation.

6

A Christian Approach to Oriental Faiths

R. W. F. WOOTTON

THE PRESENCE IN BRITAIN TODAY OF NEARLY A MILLION PEOPLE professing one or other of the faiths whose origin is in India offers a great evangelistic opportunity to Christians. But it is an opportunity only to be approached with very careful mental and spiritual preparation. Sometimes British Christians have launched out with little understanding of the faith of the people to whom they were going, and thus have left an impression of ignorance and arrogance which only repelled. We must approach our Asian neighbours with great respect. We must see them first as people who are precious in the sight of God – people with a social, economic and cultural life in which we are bound to be interested if we really care for them. We must see them also as men of faith, following traditions which have sustained their ancestors through the centuries and give meaning to life for millions today.

We need to study these faiths carefully, with minds open to all that is good and true in them. We shall not of course be blind to whatever is false or inadequate (eg. idolatry in Hinduism), but will remember that missionary writers in the past have often dwelt too much on these aspects and too little on the positive sides. We may well find much to admire in the Hindu's reverence for life and search for peace, in the Buddhist's longing for enlightenment and moral excellence and in the Sikh's practical goodness to those in need, and be challenged in our own faith and practice thereby. Such discoveries should not astonish us, for after all the eternal Word who was incarnate once for all in the Lord Jesus is also 'The light which enlightens every man' in greater or less degree (John 1:9), and the one thing which is unique in Christianity is Christ himself.

There must be a grasp of the other faith before there can be any real communication. Otherwise we shall be using terms which mean one thing to us and something quite different to our hearers. For example, if we speak of 'salvation', our Asian friend will most probably interpret this as *moksha*, deliverance from the wheel of rebirth or transmigration into final blessedness or annihilation. We also need to know what aspects of Christianity are most likely to appeal or most likely to offend, not because we wish to distort our message to suit our hearer, but simply because it is necessary to reserve certain truths till he is ready to receive them. We will now consider the three religions separately.

1. Hinduism

At first sight Hinduism appears so utterly different from Christianity that any point of contact is impossible. But as Paul Sudhakar has written, 'The emptiness of the human soul, the lack of purpose and direction of man, the hunger for union with God, the search for a meaning for existence, the longing for peace and the unceasing search for spiritual life are some of the things that occupy the Hindu mind, and it will make a better impression if Christ can be preached with this background'. Here are three specific points where contact can be made:–

a) *The concept of God as present everywhere* and dwelling in human spirits is familiar to the Hindu. Hence St John's gospel with its teaching of the indwelling Christ (15:1–7 etc.) and of the indwelling Spirit (14:17, etc.) is especially attractive to him; not that the Hindu and Christian concepts are identical, but that there is a real point of contact here, as also with St Paul's concept of being in Christ.

b) *The idea of renunciation and self-giving* is dear to Hinduism with its rather world-denying outlook. Hence the picture of Christ's self-emptying and self-humbling even to death on the Cross evokes a response in the Hindu mind – it is no accident that Gandhi's favourite hymn was 'When I survey the wondrous Cross'. But we must remember that the Hindu will expect to see a like spirit in Christ's followers.

c) Most Hindus in Britain seem to be devotees of Krishna,

seeking to follow the way of *bhakti* or *loving devotion and personal commitment* to their Lord. Without making direct comparisons Jesus can be presented as the one who is truly worthy of such devotion, the one of whom St. Peter writes, 'You have not seen him yet you love him; and trusting in him now without seeing him, you are transported with a joy too great for words'. (1 Peter 1:8), the one whom 'we love because he first loved us' (1 John 4:19).

2. Buddhism

Here again we meet a faith which is remote from orthodox Christianity, one which is even agnostic about the existence of God. We must welcome the sublimity of its ethical system which is not without parallel in Christianity. Thus the Buddhist concept of love (*metta*) as the honest desire for the true welfare of others, free from self-interest and ready for sacrifice, clearly comes close to the *agapē* of the New Testament. The Buddhist conviction that desire, lust and greed must be banished before peace is attained, is in harmony with Christ's teaching of the need to deny oneself and take up one's cross (Mark 8:34 etc.), and of Paul's stress on putting to death the old self (Gal. 2:20, 5:24 etc.).

Further, the Buddhist has a keen sense of the frustrating and impermanent character of human life and the need to pass through many lives in striving afteer a state of blessedness. To this the Christian may well say that everything has been changed by God's entry into human life in Jesus, so that a new force is at work in the world by which men may come *now* into the presence of God through him. In *Amy Carmichael of Dohnavur* (SPCK 1953) Bishop F. Houghton records her meeting once with a devout Buddhist to whom she spoke on St Paul's words, 'If, when we were God's enemies, we were reconciled through the death of his Son, how much more, now that we are reconciled, shall we be saved by his life!' (Rom. 5:10). He replied, 'True, true, it must be true. Buddha died; we know it. How can he help us who live today? He may say, "Be good"; the power to obey he cannot give.' And he pondered the words, 'Saved by his life'. Then looking deep into her eyes he said, 'If this be so, you are as an angel from heaven to us; but if it be so, we want to see it lived; can you show it to us?'

3. Sikhism

The Christian may well find himself more at home with the Sikh, with his conviction of the oneness of God, his sense of history, his reverence for his sacred book and his stress on practical goodness. While holding to *karma* and transmigration, he believes in a sense in divine grace, for Guru Nanak said, 'By our deeds (*karma*) we get our bodies, but by God's grace the door of salvation is opened to us'. From this the Christian may seek to point his Sikh friend to the one who is himself the incarnation of grace (cf John 1:14, 1 Tim. 1:15, etc.). Further the grace of Christ may well strike a responsive note in the Sikh's mind; many of them, including three of the ten Gurus, have given their lives for their faith, and this helps them to appreciate Christ's death as a voluntary sacrifice for suffering humanity. Sikhs have a conviction of the divine Spirit inspiring writers of the Granth (the Sikh holy book), enlightening the Gurus and working in some measure in the lives of all faithful Sikhs. From this concept they may be led on to seek the Holy Spirit, the gift of the risen Christ to his people, manifested in the practical goodness and service for others which the Sikh greatly admires.

One difficulty often presents itself as we deal with these faiths – the concept of differing paths to God, equally valid for those who pursue them. Thus many Hindus will accept almost all that we say about Jesus, and then add that Krishna is for them the path to God. There is no easy answer to this deeply ingrained idea. We can point out that contradictory ideas of God cannot all be true at once, any more than contradictory doctrines of astronomy or history, and that some concepts of the divine clearly are to be rejected, e.g. that of malevolent spirits constantly needing to be placated by magic or sacrifice. We can further face our Asian friend with the universal claims of Jesus Christ and with the old dilemma 'aut Deus aut homo non bonus': either he spoke the truth and so is God or he is not even a good man – he is deceived or a deceiver; he is either Lord of all or not Lord at all.

7

A Christian Approach to Islam

MICHAEL NAZIR-ALI

THE CHRISTIAN CHURCH HAS ALWAYS, OF COURSE, BEEN engaged in dialogue and/or polemic with Islam. The 8th Century church father, St. John of Damascus, wrote two disputations against the Saracens. He himself lived under Muslim rule and had indeed served in high office under the Muslim rulers. Following closely on his heels was the Nestorian patriarch Timothy who offered a Christian apology to the Caliph Malidi. Sweetman lists eight Christian apologists between the seventh and the eleventh centuries.[1] Confrontation took place in such faraway places as the Mongol Empire in China.[2] Despite these early contacts it must be emphasized that very few conversions took place; most of the discussion went on in a fairly rarefied atmosphere and hardly touched the common people. Within the confines of the Islamic empire it was forbidden to evangelise the Muslims and so the oriental churches concentrated on survival rather than expansion.

Thus the situation became fairly static until the modern missionary movement began from the West. It is easy to criticise the oriental Christians for being 'dead' etc., but it must be urged that without the context provided by nineteenth century imperialism, missionaries from the West could hardly have begun their missionary enterprise. Muslims are deeply suspicious of mission and regard it as an appendage of the Crusades! They seem to believe that the 'Christian' West must think, 'If not by conquest then by persuasion'. Even with the imperial 'umbrella', missionaries have had very limited success in the central Islamic lands. In recent times the ancient churches of the East seem to be reviving from their slumber and in many cases there is a fruitful exchange of evangelists from one Muslim country to another. This type of person is more acceptable both to the host church and the host government because cultural domination is not feared.

Many ways have been tried to evangelise the Muslim, some of them conciliatory, others highly polemical. How should we evangelise the Muslim? The answer is simply that we must be biblical in our approach. Why? Because a) the Bible tells us how to behave towards God and man, it is, in short, our rule book, and b) the story of evangelism in the Bible is a very successful story.

Our foundation must be biblical, our disposition must be loving and our intellectual position must be honest.

Basic Assumptions

The presuppositions we start with are very important so far as the development of dialogue is concerned. If one starts with the assumption that Allah is an idol, Muhammad is anti-Christ etc., then the relationship with one's Muslim neighbour is likely to be distant at best and hostile at worst. One's first basic assumption therefore is that the Christian and the Muslim are talking about the same God. Their standpoint is different, their emphasis is different and their understanding of God's attributes is different. Nevertheless it is quite clear historically that the Muslim concept of God is continuous with the Judaeo-Christian concept. The Quran is quite explicit in this claim:

> We believe in Allah and that which was sent down on us and that which was sent down on Abraham, Ishmael, Isaac, Jacob, and the Tribes (of Israel) and that which was given to Moses and to Jesus and that which was given to all the prophets from their Lord. We do not discriminate between any of them and to him (i.e. Allah) we have surrendered (*Quran II:137*).

Even if this were not so, it is quite clear that the early Christians adopted *theos* for 'god' from their pagan Hellenistic environs and the Western church later adopted *deus* from the pagan Roman usage. It is true that the early Christians did not identify their God with the Greek or Roman pantheon but this was primarily due to the polytheistic character of Greek and Roman religion. Paul, in Acts 17, has no hesitation in using the praise of God spoken (as they understood him) by Greek poets who were regarded as inspired! However, it should be made plain that one is *starting* with Islam's idea of God, not *finishing* with it. The task of the evangelist is to develop and build on this view of God.

The second basic assumption is that in addition to the Bible the Christian will use the Quran and other Islamic literature to press home his argument. The Quran contains much that is useful and we must not reject it all completely. On the other hand it has much that is of doubtful value and therefore it must be used very discriminately. We have already seen that Paul was not afraid to quote from what may be called pagan 'scripture' when the occasion demanded (Acts 17:28, Titus 1:12).

The third basic assumption is that we should treat belief in the One God as a preparation for the Gospel, i.e. the Muslim belief is to be considered one advance on mere paganism and polytheism. What precisely is meant by a preparation? The answer comes surprisingly from an Urdu Rubaij of Mantana Altaf Husain Hali:

> 'The Hindu discovered thy glory in his idol, the Zoroastrians sing thy praises over the fire, the materialist was driven to thee from the fact of the Universe. No-one could formulate a coherent denial of thee'.[3]

What is meant here is not an easy syncretism but, that from his inadequate attempts at understanding God man is constantly driven to the Reality. Surely this agrees with Acts 14:17: ' . . . yet he did not leave himself without witness'. In Romans too Paul affirms that God is known by all peoples however much they have corrupted their knowledge of him and however much they have been permeated with idolatry (Rom. 1:20–23).

With these three assumptions we can examine some of the issues at stake in Christian – Muslim dialogue.

Issues at Stake

a) *God*: The Muslim view of God is that God is utterly transcendent, his relation to the world and to men is that of Creator to creatures. A Persian poet puts it like this:

> *The Jealousy of God surely means that he is utterly Other,*
> *He is beyond discourse and the noise of words.*[4]

Although God is spoken of as loving man in the Quran (*Quran* V:54: 'He loves them' [i.e. his people], yet God's love is almost detached approval for the good. He is merciful to sinners, but not loving. In any case the radical love of God found in the New Testament is entirely absent in Islam and the whole concept of a God who suffers for his people is quite foreign.

In approaching a Muslim it is quite useful to start from God's omnipotence. Here there is common ground and the Christian can then ask the Muslim why if God is omnipotent does the Muslim think it impossible for him to become man. This is a very difficult point in the discussion because the Muslim will immediately ask who, if God became man, would be left to rule the universe? It is here that one gets tangled up in all sorts of talk about 'parts' of God etc. I think that the Christian position can be stated thus: God has tried down the ages to speak through the prophets; however the prophets were not really successful in getting the message across, so God decided to speak to man himself through a human form, Jesus therefore was God speaking to man and yet he was fully human. He is therefore God's Word (*Quran* IV:172).

b) *The Trinity:* This of course is the most misunderstood Christian doctrine in the Quran. Here is usually the first objection to Christianity brought by the Muslim and yet it is advisable to steer clear of it for a while and to lay the foundation of basic Christian truths that lie behind the doctrine of the Trinity. When pressed by the Muslim, perhaps one can say something like this: 'The Christian along with others knows that God is the Creator of the world and is its Sustainer. This is God the Father, Father because he brings us into being and provides for our needs. The Christian knows that God has spoken in the life, death and resurrection of Jesus. This is God the Son, Son not in any physical sense but as the eternal word of God he proceeds from the Father. The Muslim understands the concept of the eternal word of God and it should be not too difficult to show him how Jesus is the eternal word of the Father. One can talk about his authoritative preaching, his raising of people from the dead, his powers of creation, all powers explicitly mentioned in the Quran (II:87, III:49).

The Holy Spirit is the agency used by God the Father to work in the church and in the world. He is known through his power and the Quran is aware of his existence (II:87, XVII:86, XL:15 etc.). Muslim commentators generally try to identify the Holy Spirit with Gabriel but I can find little warrant for this in the Quran itself.

c) *The Death of Jesus:* The Quran is ambiguous about the death of Jesus but in any case the Atonement is explicitly rejected as a doctrine. How should one talk about Jesus' death to the Muslim? Two approaches may be useful here:

i. To say that man was created as obedient to God and yet free. He chose to rebel and was neither able nor willing as a result of sin to return to God. Christ came to do what man could not and would not do, i.e. to be a perfectly obedient man, to be the second Adam. Thus in God's sight Man was seen in Christ to return to obedience. Christians are those who have been accepted *on trust* by God as obedient because of their faith in Christ's work and because of their willingness to follow Christ. Christ's radical obedience to God led inevitably to a clash with evil men and with evil forces and finally to his crucifixion; he had been obedient unto death. There is an analogy to Christ's obedience in Muslim martyrology: the example of Hassan and Hussein in refusing to surrender to infidelity and dying for their belief. However, Christ was openly vindicated by God and raised up on the third day.

ii. Christ's death and resurrection are a battle with the devil and set man free from the slavery of sin. Jesus Christ therefore is a revelation from God, i.e. he shows us that God *is*. God in Christ is not just a beautiful concept, he is real and can be seen, touched and handled. He is also the perfectly obedient Man and restores man to a relationship of trust with God. He is the Saviour because God accepts us because of his perfect obedience and because in following him we are saved.

d) *Jesus and the Quran*: In discussion with the Muslim it should be noted that Muhammad is *not* the word of God, it is the Quran that is the word of God. Therefore it is the Quran's claim to be the word of God which must be compared to Jesus' claims. On the one hand one can stress the authority of Jesus Christ, his miracles, his resurrection, and on the other, one can, with sensitivity, question the accuracy of the Quran, its moral teaching etc. This is a matter of deep study and cannot of course be discussed within the confines of a brief paper.

e) *Jesus and Muhammad*: Although Muhammad is not considered the word of God, he is the founder of Islam and his life can be compared to the life of Jesus. The pure life of Jesus is incomparably greater that the relatively worldly life of Muhammad. This again is a matter for detailed study. One must not, of course, engage in a mud-slinging match but point out that even according to the Quran, Muhammad is a worldly man involved in fighting, in taking wives, in raiding and pilfering, whereas Jesus is free from these preoccupations and leads a life of nearness to God and compassion to his neighbour. Which is the more obviously godly way?

f) *Incarnation in Islam*: Bishop Cragg has suggested that the idea of 'sentness' could be a starting point for Muslim – Christian discussion in this field. He points out that the very fact of God's speaking through his messengers involves God in the world. Is it so far-fetched, one may then ask the Muslim, that God speaks through a certain man in such a unique and immediate way so that we can say this is God with us? It is to be noted that Islam has rarely managed to keep free of incarnational language. Very early on in Islamic history we find incarnational language being used of Muhammad. The sufis, of course, used incarnational language not only about Muhammad but very often about themselves and about other sufis. All this despite the prohibition of incarnational language!

Can the Christian not point the Muslim to him who claimed to be the incarnate Son of God and the power of whose life confirmed this claim? In any case, instances of incarnational language used by Muslims are useful in showing Muslims that the concept is not utterly strange to their tradition.

g) *Salvation*: The Quran acknowledges Jesus to be the Messiah, the Saviour, but in truth there is no saviour figure in Islam. Salvation is obtained by heeding the prophets of God and by performing good works. In practice however, Muslims, like other men, feel inadequate and feel that they need God's grace for forgiveness and salvation. It is then possible to talk to the Muslim about the work of Christ outlined in (c).

h) *The Bible*: The Muslim has many misconceptions about the Bible and has both Quranic and traditional warrant for believing that it has been distorted by both Jews and Christians (II:80 etc.). The Muslim believes that the various sections of the Bible, the Torah, the Psalms, the Gospel (sic) were given directly from God to the relevant prophet. One has to explain to him therefore that the Bible was written by many men over hundreds of years all writing under God's inspiration. One can point out that very ancient manuscripts of the Bible exist and that if the Muslim thinks that the Bible has been substantially altered then proof can be given against this. Muslims have recently discovered the work of biblical critics and point to that as evidence that the Bible has been changed. Whatever the merits of any particular example of criticism, we can point out that criticism is equipped to discover the origins of various parts of scripture and not to discover whether a particular document is a substitute for another. Furthermore, scholars have shown that the central books of the N.T. are very early and that the story they present is consistent given certain variations in detail and emphasis. The central facts remain unchanged, that Jesus Christ lived a most remarkable life, that he died a tragic death and that he was gloriously raised from the dead. Certainly, when the Quran is examined under the very same canons as employed in biblical criticism it hardly emerges as a unity. It has various strands of Jewish, Christian and pagan traditions. It has different versions of the same story, it has unlikely genealogies etc. Furthermore, it has attached to it the doctrine of abrogation by which earlier

Quranic revelations are abrogated if they contradict later ones! This is of course a very convenient doctrine because if one points to a contradiction in the Quran the Muslim can always claim that the later revelation abrogates the earlier.

One must explain to the Muslim that the formation of the N.T. Canon was a gradual process. Different authorities existed testifying to the life of Christ; the church had to gather these together, and it is quite obvious that in their central claims they bear each other out.

Certain beliefs in Islam appear to arise from an appreciation of God as manifested in nature. Other beliefs seem to arise from a definite experience of God – a *mysterium tremendum et fascinans*.[5] These experiences seem to be genuine and they should be accepted by the Christian. Is the Quran inspired? I think that the Christian would have to say, No. There is much in the Quran which contradicts the Christian records and one cannot say that to the Christian it sounds like God speaking to man. Nevertheless it does indicate a genuine experience of God and a desire to live according to God's will; as such it must be respected by all men and Christians particularly.

Apart from the special approach outlined above, it must be remembered that the Muslim is just like any other human being and shares the predicament of the human race. As such he has the same anxieties and needs that all of us have. The Gospel can be preached to the Muslim as to anyone else, as answering man's deepest need for forgiveness, for wholeness, for knowledge of God. The above is merely an attempt to discuss some of the special problems that Muslims face when confronted with the Gospel. It is our task to remove unnecessary stumbling-blocks from the way of the Muslim searching for truth.

NOTES

1 J. W. Sweetman, *Islam and Christian Theology* Vol. 66. (Lutterworth. 1945).
2 R. W. Souther, *Western View of Islam in the Middle Ages*, (Harvard 1962).
3 Ruba'ijab-E-Hali OUP 1932 p. 1f.
4 Mathnawi I 1713.

5 This phrase was used by Rudolf Otto (1869 – 1937) to point up some basic elements in religious experience. God is experienced as *mysterium*, a mystery, because he is entirely different from man, a reality which cannot be apprehended. God is *tremendum*, causing trembling or fear, an overwhelming sense of awe. Yet he is also *fascinans*, attracting the worshipper not only with the promise of future blessing but as the infinitely gracious source of all good.

8

A Christian Approach to Jews

GORDON JESSUP

SOME CHRISTIANS HAVE A VERY LOW OPINION OF JEWS; OTHERS, aware of God's care and purpose for his chosen people, put them 'on a pedestal'. Jewish people know that if God has chosen them, it is for special responsibility rather than special favour – and want only to be treated as human beings, neither more nor less! Our Christian responsibility is to offer the Gospel to every human being.

Jews are becoming Christians in increasing numbers. Some Christians believe that evangelism among them is unnecessary because 'all Israel will be saved' when the Lord returns. They should ask themselves why, then, the Holy Spirit is working in Jewish hearts today. The following considerations are worth bearing in mind when we think about Jews turning to Christ.

A Christian Priority

A Jew becomes a Christian: his people have known, for centuries, the feeling of being an unpopular minority in an alien society: who better, then, to help today's church come to terms with the similar role which sometimes seems to be its future?

Consider the special gifts of the Jewish people: their spiritual insights, their special abilities in artistic, scientific, commercial and other realms. Covet the talents of a gifted people for Jesus!

The church's strategy for outreach must include the Jews, for the church's own sake! God promised Abram (Genesis 12:3), concerning his descendants, 'I will bless those who bless you.' The greatest blessing we can offer a Jew is our supreme treasure, the Gospel – thus receiving for ourselves a blessing according to the promise.

God also said, 'Him who curses you I will curse,' and we may expect spiritual deadness in the church to appear side by side with neglect of our missionary obligation towards the Jewish people.

Most Jews are aware that 'Christians' have persecuted their people many times, in many ways, in many places, for many centuries. Past oppressions of Jewish people and communities are another reason for placing the Jews high on our list of evangelistic priorities. For too long, Christians have presented their Jewish neighbours with a lying testimony. In those who should have been showing them the love of Jesus, they have seen bitterness and hate, or at least dislike. We must at last tell the Jews the truth about Jesus!

A Christian Attitude

We cannot expect the Jew to distinguish 'real' from 'nominal' Christians. The church as a whole is guilty. Many see Christianity, especially Christian evangelism, as a threat to their Jewish identity. Some of their ancestors were coerced into conversion; they are therefore suspicious of Christians trying to 'convert' them. So we approach the Jew with humility, carefully avoiding things which will appear as threats or as bitter reminders. For example, wearing a cross seems harmless enough – but it is the sign under which Jews have been persecuted. And beware of Jewish jokes! Jews often tell them, but, told by a Gentile, the same joke may be, or sound, anti-Jewish.

A Jew may equate 'becoming a Christian' with 'turning traitor': family and friends are likely to reject him if he does. The Jewish Christian is likely to face a crisis of identity.

The proper Christian attitude to Jews combines love and sympathetic understanding with real sorrow for the shameful treatment of them in the past. Jewish people still need the Saviour. But we must in no way 'push' our beliefs at them. By God's grace we have a personal relationship with him, which our Jewish neighbour also needs – but persuasion is the Holy

Spirit's task. Just let him make use of the testimony of our life and words, as he wills.

So the Christian approach to Jews involves humility, understanding, and never pressure.

We have a debt, as Christians, to the Jewish people: Jesus, with a Jewish mother, Jewish upbringing, Jewish nationality, Jewish disciples, Jewish teachings, fulfilled promises made to the Jew's ancestors and recorded in Jewish Scriptures. Nearly all the New Testament writers were Jews, as were several thousand founder-members of the Christian Church – and so on! 'Salvation is from the Jews' (John 4:22). I must not approach the Jew as if I alone possess all truth – there is no room for the least hint of a patronising attitude on our part. The Gospel we offer is ours by God's grace, not because we are 'special'.

Besides, there is much that we can learn from the Jew and his people. Many Jewish observances are fascinating, and helpful for the understanding of Christian things. Ignorant, perhaps, of Jewish customs and observances, we can use even ignorance as basis for questions through which a friendly relationship can develop. As in other areas of evangelism, a question leading to discussion is better than a sermon; discussing 'religion' may lead to opportunities for talk about spiritual matters.

A Christian Approach

As we get to know the Jewish people, so as to witness effectively, we shall learn to avoid false assumptions. It does not follow that someone who is Jewish is necessarily religious. He *may* believe that personal religious experience is important; he may even be searching for more. But he *may* feel that religion is irrelevant, or be atheist or agnostic. He may perhaps view the Bible as fine Jewish literature, containing noble ethical ideals, but with no special authority over his beliefs or way of life.

But we cannot assume that someone 'not very religious' is therefore not very Jewish. He may neither understand his own religion well, nor perhaps admit any obligation to it – yet he may feel a need to maintain his Jewish identity. Community membership, family and cultural heritage, support for Israel – these and other things may make him aware and proud of his Jewishness. He may accept the moral and social values of his heritage, and be deeply involved in contemporary causes.

There is much 'common ground' on which Jew and Christian may meet and build friendship: social concern; moral values; interest in Jewish culture or the land of Israel; the nature of God and how to reach him; common concern for persecuted co-religionists in Eastern Europe or elsewhere. (A Jewish acquaintance may not understand Christian lack of concern for threatened Israel, or for the plight of Russian Jews.)

We should not be afraid to move on, from 'common ground' to areas of difference. If the occasion arises naturally, we shall testify to what our faith means to us, what the Lord has done and is doing for us. But let us use ordinary, everyday English! Many of the 'technical terms' of religion are meaningless to non-Christians; to the Jew they may even have an entirely different meaning. 'Conversion' is what Christians have tried to do to their people, often forcibly, in the past. 'Redemption', if it means anything apart from trading stamps or pawnshops, means the coming of Messiah or the Messianic Age – not the Christian's idea of personal salvation. 'Missionary', or the names of evangelistic agencies working among Jews, may suggest the idea that Jews are heathens who need converting.

'Christ' is the title under which his people have been persecuted; it is also the Greek equivalent of 'Messiah', and to use it in conversation with a Jew may be premature as well as offensive. 'Jesus', a personal name, is usually (though not invariably) acceptable. Note that many Jews no longer expect a personal Messiah, while still looking for the Messianic Age.

If a Jewish contact is religiously committed and observant, he will probably know more of rabbinic tradition and Prayer Book than of the Bible. Some Jews know the Scriptures well, most do not. (Try not to call it 'Old' Testament!) Modern Judaism has developed considerably from the Judaism of the Bible. It is a pattern of living, covering every part of life, based on the Torah (the books Genesis to Deuteronomy *as interpreted* through the ages by the rabbis). Those first five books, especially, are the actual words of God; the oral traditions of the rabbis are equally authoritative.

Judaism emphasises right action rather than right belief. It makes no distinction between secular and sacred: the food laws are as important as the prayer laws.

Judaism today is interpreted in different ways by Orthodox, Reform, and Liberal groups. All agree in denying the doctrines of the Trinity and the Deity of Christ. Some Jews see in Jesus a great religious reformer. Others think of him as an Orthodox Jew, a rabbi, or as a political revolutionary, a false Messiah, or a minor prophet.

This is not enough! The Christian wants his Lord to receive all the honour due to him: he came to be Messiah, Saviour, King of the Jews. Jews may find it hard to believe, but he is eternal Son of God, the Word become flesh. Most Jews have not rejected Jesus – either he is irrelevant, or they have rejected the inadequate image of him which the Church by its behaviour and teachings has presented. With humility and patience, love and understanding, we must let the Jewish people know who he really is.

Initial rejection of the message will not destroy our friendship and concern. We shall await patiently the next Spirit-given opportunity, remembering that the most effective witness is an increasingly Christ-like life.

9

Christian Approaches to People of Other Faiths in School

MAURICE HOBBS

An Important Comparison

'CHRISTIAN APPROACHES' IN WHAT MIGHT BE DESCRIBED AS 'free space' are one thing: inside an institution, and that a compulsory one, they are quite another.

'Free Space'
In the 'free space' of parks or streets, people of other faiths are able to accept, avoid or reject, the approaches of Christians with booklets or Bibles. They may, or may not, accept the approaches of 'fishermen' outside churches just before the evening service. They can, and frequently do, open the door to strangers who knock, with a smile and a message, but they need not. They are able to decide the length of a conversation, and whether they want to meet again for another talk. They can respond, eagerly or otherwise, to the approaches of Christian neighbours with offers of help in difficult circumstances – though few are the Christians who actually live in the same areas as people of other faiths, near enough to make real neighbourliness possible.

All these are *voluntary approaches between adults* whose rights are respected in both directions. They are mainly *individual*, though groups of people like Bible college students may engage in area-wide 'tracting', and open-air work. And they are *on more or less equal terms*, with respect on either side. Such approaches are *defined in religious terms*, as 'evangelism' or 'outreach with the Gospel', and that means almost by definition, *limited in duration*, because undertaken in free time (except when the Christians concerned are missionaries, and there are few of them); and *limited in scope*, since the aim is to 'save souls'. Even if entry into full church-membership is the ultimate aim, the scope of the approach is still limited in terms of social intercourse across cultural boundaries, for the church meets most completely only once a week for an hour or so.

'Inside an institution'
The school situation is different. *The encounter is not voluntary*, however pleasant a teacher may try to make it, or however much a child may desire education. *The encounter is not between equals*, but between adults and children; adults who have 'authority' from their academic status and training, and 'power' to reward and punish, to choose and employ children, who are usually less knowledgeable and physically weaker. *The encounter is much less limited in duration and scope*. It amounts not merely to a brief session on a door-step, but to 6 hours or so, 5 days a week, for 12 or 13 weeks of each of 33 terms over the 11 years period of compulsory schooling.

Christian approaches

During the child's long school career, Christian approaches of some kind will be made to him in three different modes:

1. *Most generally, in the total curriculum*, which includes not only the content of subjects like History or Literature, but also the rules about conduct and corporate living applied to corridors, dining-hall and games-field.
2. *Most obviously, in School or House Assemblies, and in R.E. lessons*.
3. *Most evangelistically*, (and probably, most Evangelically) *in out-of-school activities*, such as meetings of Christian fellowships etc., in the lunch-hour.

These three modes must be examined separately, but in all three, while children may meet some teachers who will really approach them with the Gospel, they will also encounter some others whose beliefs and commitment are undistinguishable from those prevailing in the general population. In the essay that follows I propose to adopt the device of Salley and Behm, in their book *Your God is too White* (Lion, 1975), and use the term 'Christian' with a capital C to mean those who are truly committed to Christ, and 'christian' with a small 'c' for those who are only culturally Christian, or indeed, post-Christian. Evangelicals may be able to make this distinction without too much difficulty, but people of other faiths are much more likely to label all white teachers as 'christians'. In any case, it is all too easy for a Christian teacher to be 'conformed to the world', the world of staff-room attitudes, which may or may not be favourable to coloured children – particularly if he is the only Christian on the staff. Thus a distinctive Christian approach may not be easily recognised, but will seem blurred, even compromised.

'*Most generally, in the total curriculum*'
The total curriculum of schools is a resultant of many factors, which have been at work over centuries, but which in the short-term include:

> the philosophy of head-teachers and staff – itself reflecting their own education and training
> the policies of local councils, both the elected committee-men and full-time professional administrators
> the influence of parents and public opinion generally.

In spite of the jealously guarded local and professional autonomy of L.E.A.s and teachers, which has produced considerable variety in responses to the presence of 'immigrant' children in our schools, it is possible to talk in general terms of the curriculum. For all these people in all schools and localities have been brought up within a coherent set of beliefs and values and practices, which is sometimes described as Western Civilization, White Anglo-Saxon Protestant culture or the British Way of Life. And this cultural base is reflected in the curriculum.

In our history, we have been schooled by the Elizabethan Religious Settlement and by the Book of Common Prayer. The Bible in English has been a veritable text-book for our people, so that many can use its language without acknowledging the source. So great has been the influence of the universities (originally ecclesiastical foundations) and the churches generally, in the development of education in Britain, that schools, as the institutions responsible for initiating newcomers into society – whether born here or immigrants – present to all children a 'world-view', which is deeply imbued with Christian values, couched often in Christian terms and embodied in Christian images. These are quite often stated overtly, particularly in Roman Catholic schools, which incidentally take in very few children of other faiths. But they are also strongly present in what is sometimes called the 'hidden curriculum' in maintained schools, and are mediated through subjects such as Literature, History, Music, etc., as well as R.E. (of which, more later).

Some teachers, even in these latter days, may still think of the school as a 'microcosm of the kingdom of God', Christian, benevolent, ordered, whole. Even those who reject Christianity usually believe in the general rightness of what they do in schools – and, in spite of the 'progressive methods' and 'permissiveness', of which schools are often accused, the majority of children in this country are educated in traditional values and lesson content, in traditional ways. Few schools have made any far-reaching changes in organisation, content or methods in response to the presence of children of other faiths. Yet, 'the classroom is the one place in the country where Christians, real and nominal, and Muslims, Sikhs or Hindus, meet regularly and continuously, at close quarters and compulsorily.' [1]

All this being the case, children of other faiths will grow up with an image of Christianity shaped largely by what they have learned in school, but interpreted through the thought-forms of their own faith and culture.

Thus, the total curriculum is in general terms a 'christian approach' to children of other faiths, even though some Evangelical Christians may think it to be compromised and defective, rationalistic and diffuse, progressive in the wrong direction. It may well – and rightly – be argued that 'Christian approaches', as defined by Evangelicals, are not really involved, and indeed are not possible, within much that goes on in the long process of compulsory schooling. Nevertheless, the child of Muslim or Sikh parentage can hardly be expected to make the distinction. It is, therefore, essential that those who make 'Christian approaches' in 'free space' to young people who appear to be of other faiths should realise that they have to deal with the pre-suppositions, not only of those other faiths but of impressions of 'christianity' received in school.

To people from overseas, Britain may well be simply 'the home of the missionaries', hence a Christian country, and they are unlikely to realise the compromises that are embodied in the curriculum of schools in a secularised, though historically Christian, society. Their expectations may be of two kinds: that here ideal Christianity will be embodied, particularly in the teacher-pupil relationship; or, they may be realist enough to see that in Britain, Christianity is more honoured in the breach than the observance, and conclude that it is somehow the ideology of the 'haves' operating to persuade the 'have-nots' to be content with their lot. In either case, the 'christian' approaches in the general sense of what goes on in school may bring disillusion and disappointment.

It is not, however, merely in the matter of unfulfilled expectations that this generalised 'christian' approach must be examined, but also in relation to attitudes towards ethnic minorities. For instance, many people – and teachers are no exception – continue to use the word 'immigrants', even the grammatically impossible 'second-generation immigrant' – for the children of other faiths in school. Thus these new citizens may be seen as perpetual strangers and as an 'alien wedge' – and the most convinced of Christians may be the most concerned at their presence as constituting a threat to Christian England. In such a case, the 'approach', friendly as it may be to individuals, is in fact rejection, and with the heightened awareness of child-hood, the children soon detect the 'double-think'.

Unconsciously we may denigrate the culture in which the child has received his earliest and most effective socialisation; we may obliterate the history of his people, without permitting him truly to share our own; we may lead him into personal crises of identity. Since so much of our history has been concerned with the conquest of the Indian sub-continent and Africa, our text-books may be full of images of Muslims, Sikhs and Hindus which are unflattering, if not hostile. More pages may be devoted to the exploits of Clive of India than to the missionary activities of William Carey. How, then, will Asian children arrive at a true understanding of Christianity and of the Christian approaches that are made to them?

Yet, great as its influence obviously is, the school is remote from the home-life of the children of other faiths. Much closer will be the mosque or gurdwara, because linked with the traditional culture and world view, forming part of the framework of ritual and values within which the family life of Muslims and Sikhs has long been fashioned. In school, strangers to their faith and history will ignore or interpret those values, rituals and history from the point of view of an imperial, metropolitan and missionary island; in mosque and gurdwara the same events may be spoken or sung about from the point of view of the colonised and the exiles. Clearly, then, the child is placed in a quandary, challenged by two 'truths', the British and his own. In such uncertainty there may be an opening for the Truth himself (see John 14:6). But, if he, the Lord Christ, is to be realised he must be presented in ways which are uncluttered by matters which are not specifically 'of Christ', but of the British Way of Life and Western culture.

'Most obviously, in ... Assemblies, and in R.E. lessons'

The 1944 Education Act specified an 'act of collective worship on the part of all pupils' every day, and regular religious instruction. It did not specify the kind of worship or in what religious tradition it should be. In 1944 it was simply assumed that these activities would be Christian, and that the Bible would be the main text-book. On the face of things this would seem to constitute a Christian approach, but even in 1944 things were not so simple, and since then there have been many changes, some of which have been motivated by the presence of children of other faiths in schools; but not all, because change in what is taught by what methods has taken place equally in schools where there are no such pupils.

It is not possible to understand fully these changes nor the realities of 'Christian approaches to people of other faiths in school' within the field of this statutory requirement without understanding certain historical developments.

Implicit in the royal title, 'Defender of the Faith' is a 'confessional state'. Originally 'singular', having only one form of confession, the 'established' church, it has now become 'plural', with not one church, but many denominations, all confessing Christianity and all acceptable to the state, if not in fact co-opted into its structures. More than that, 'liberty for tender consciences', which began as a purely Christian concept, has been extended to cover the rights of people of all religious confessions or none.

This process, which began in the seventeenth century, was accelerated in the nineteenth, by the battles between the established church and the nonconformists about the nature of religious teaching in the new state system of schools. A landmark in the process is the celebrated 'Cowper-Temple clause' in the Education Act of 1870, which forbade the teaching of denominational dogma. The process was reinforced by the establishment of the Indian Empire in 1858. That Empire could not be a 'confessional state', though missionary activity was permitted, if not sponsored. Instead of discrimination in favour of any one religious group its posture had to be one of neutrality and 'indifferentism', even though the Emperor would continue to be 'Head of the Church' in England.

In Britain, the establishment of compulsory schooling both signalled and hastened the decline of the confessional state. Yet, to maintain social cohesion, all states require a system of organising values and norms to be accepted by all citizens; and nowhere is such a system more necessary than in a society which rejects the use of force in directing and controlling its people. A national system of compulsory schooling is the obvious instrument by which such a 'civil religion' can be inculcated. In a 'confessional state' the schools will train the future citizens according to the doctrines and morality of its 'civil religion', whether it be Islam or Communism or Christianity. In a state which 'confesses' toleration or 'indifferentism', there may be no overt statements of national goals or values, but still the schools will convey that 'civil religion' to their pupils. By such a process, immigrants will be led 'when in Rome to do what the Romans do', though the accommodation may never be complete, and there may be, by reaction, a reinforcement of cultural consciousness.

In Britain, with our history, it is obvious that the values and normative histories of Christianity will continue to form a large part of the teaching of the 'civil religion' of a state which has in reality ceased to be 'confessional'. Yet this poses several serious questions:

1. How far can this residual christianity be equated with the Gospel of Our Lord and Saviour Jesus Christ? How far does it obscure the real message?
2. How far can that Gospel be the servant of political purposes such as the maintenance of social cohesion?
3. How far can that Gospel be offered to people of other faiths as part of the 'civil religion', and what are the rights of citizens in a democracy to bring up their children in their chosen or inherited faith?
4. What happens to our concept of conversion as the response of love to Love, made freely and not under constraint, if the children are a captive audience?

These questions are not new and were debated long before there were any Hindu or Muslim children in British schools. Three solutions had already been arrived at. The dual system of education enabled independent schools, separate from the state system, and the 'aided' schools within it, to continue to be more or less 'confessional', and parents who could afford to do so were able to take advantage of this arrangement. Minorities, such as Roman Catholics and Jews, were permitted to withdraw their children from assemblies and Religious Instruction. Thirdly, teachers adopted pragmatic solutions which involved stress upon History (of Old Testament heroes) or Geography (of the Mediterranean basin) within the agreed syllabuses, and either increasing syncretism in content or gradual abandonment of the attempt to teach religion at all, substituting Moral Education.

Few 'immigrant' parents withdraw their children, perhaps because they do not know that they have the right to do so, or perhaps because they do not wish to lose the opportunity of hearing and using the English language or of receiving any educative experience. Many Asian children do well in the Religious Knowledge examinations, perhaps because this is a form of knowledge which has a genuine appeal for them. Whatever the case, it is clear that they do not regard such instruction as threatening any of their own faith or culture, while giving them access to the British way of life.

In this way they are aligned with those teachers who believe that a knowledge of Christianity is essential to a proper understanding of British history and literature, and that such knowledge is part of a proper academic discipline to be taught and studied on the same footing as other subjects. For them the presentation of the Gospel would be incidental to the study of the historical development of the faith and of a country deeply influenced by it. Any teaching that was distinctively spiritual or doctrinal would, on this argument, have to be left to the churches, and this is what happens in practice.

This duty to educate their own children in a particular faith has been left by the state schools very largely to parents and institutions of the Muslim or Sikh communities. Though some teachers may discover very real ignorance of their own faith on the part of young Muslims or Hindus, this reflects the accommodations which their parents have had to make with life in a foreign country, in many cases in the absence of the institutional support on which they would rely at home. However, teachers also complain of the weariness caused to the children by long hours of instruction by rote, in a language they do not understand which many children undergo at the mosque after school hours. This suggests that the communities are at pains to make good the omission of teaching about their faith in the schools.

This omission might be justified on the grounds that it is more essential to lead the children into the ways of their adopted country – ways which, incidentally, may violate the laws of their own faith, in the use of alcohol, for instance, or in making the dog, an unclean animal to Muslims, 'a man's best friend'.

Yet there are teachers who for 'professional' reasons have introduced readings from the Qu'ran or the Gita in assemblies, and have drawn up syllabuses of comparative religion. It is good teaching method to 'begin where the children are' and to 'go from the known to the unknown'. To ignore a child's cultural roots, or to obliterate his people's history, may do him psychological harm by leading him to a 'negative self-image'.[2]

For whatever reason, it seems to be true that more changes have occurred in R.E. syllabuses to prepare 'pupils for life in a multiracial society', than in, say, English Literature, History or Geography. (Schools Council Working Paper 50, *Multiracial Education: need and innovation*, is of great interest on this matter.) It may be that teachers of R.E. are more sensitive to the needs of children – that could be expected certainly of followers of the Lord Jesus; it may be that, in natural justice, some recognition could not be denied to other faiths with a numerous following among children in school. More cynically, it may be that changes have somehow been accepted in a subject of low status (R.E. frequently has only the minimum time allowance) and of peripheral importance, leaving the other subjects to go on as before.

The trend of this discussion has been to render problematic the reality, as well as the possibility, of 'Christian Approaches to children of other faiths', both through the general curriculum and through those activities specifically labelled Religious Education. Much, of course, depends upon what counts as a 'Christian approach', and much upon the aims we have in mind when an approach is made.

It could be argued that by loosening the ties of the old order and by introducing children of other faiths to the beliefs, customs and values of a Christian country of long-standing, schools are, in fact, making an encounter with the Risen Christ easier for them. This is, surely, to claim too much for the Christian-ness of present-day Britain and to give too little weight to the familiarity of Asian people with living in multi-faith situations, and to the attractions of secular society for those who are newly emancipated from the close ties of their traditional cultures.

Many Christians would argue that only in school do most children have the opportunity to hear of Jesus and his love, and therefore the traditional Christian syllabuses should be maintained, even strengthened. But we have, I think, to face the awkward fact that national and individual commitment to Christ had declined during, and in spite of, years of compulsory 'christian' Religious Education. It could be argued that this is because the subject has been badly taught, yet a great deal of thought and prayer has been devoted, by sincere, convinced and competent Christian teachers to the development of syllabuses, lessons and assembly programmes. And still the children say they are 'boring' – white children probably more often than Asians. This is a fact that deserves attention by researchers who are also teachers and theologians.

'Most evangelistically ... in out-of-school activities'

Often the most sincere, effective and personal Christian activities take place in the lunch-hour and after school. (The same thing is also true of Music.)

At Christian Union, club or discussion group – and there are many varieties of all these – attendance is voluntary, and children are frequently able to 'do their own thing' in organising and conducting their own meetings. They may be helped and stimulated by Christian members of staff, or by the travelling secretaries of the Inter-Schools Christian Fellowship, but increasingly these have a supporting and advisory role, rather than a supervisory one. Free-lance evangelists and representatives of local churches and house-groups may be invited to one or more meetings.

Under these circumstances the claims of Christ may be put freely before the children and decisions appealed for – but some head teachers are sensitive to the possibility of complaint from parents of too strong pressure for conversion, particularly from one religion to another. In some cases the words and methods of certain groups have led to stricter controls and even the vetoing of afterschool Christian activities.

The great question in the context of this Commission is, however, how far these out-of-school activities are likely to be effective as approaches to Muslim, Sikh or Hindu children. Research is necessary to determine the actual numbers of Asian children who might attend, but the Inter-Schools Christian Fellowship has recently designated one travelling secretary, Miss Margaret Owen, to work particularly in this field.

My impression is that not many Asian children do in fact participate and for many reasons. First, there is the increasing segregation of 'black' children in certain schools and inner city areas, from which white Christians have already migrated. As a result there are few Christian children in the schools to which Asian children go, to initiate the kind of activities under discussion. Increasingly, we may expect that West Indian children will take these initiatives, with the increasing growth of 'black' Evangelical churches in the neighbourhood of these schools. For this we can thank God, at the same time admitting that these churches have their own problems with the young people, who in school may be taught to think for themselves and question the authority of parents and pastors; admitting also that the relationships between West Indian Christians and their 'heathen' neighbours may be embittered by competition for jobs and scarce housing, and made difficult by the variety of languages involved in the multi-faith situation.

Another factor which operates against the participation of Asian children is the fact that many, if not most, go home at lunch-time, and that strict families require that their girls shall be escorted by their brothers to and fro. Unless both children wish to attend, neither can. Similar restrictions apply to school expeditions and camps.

Even so, there is no doubt that the children are anxious to share in any truly educative experience and many are willing to engage in serious discourse on religious matters. Serious consideration needs to be given to the terms and topics of such discourse. Does a Christian approach include listening to a Muslim point of view and according it respect? Can it start from somewhere within Sikhism and lead both Christian and Sikh participants to a greater understanding of the Lord Jesus, his Person and his Work? If in fact the effective Christian approaches to Hindus and others are to be made after school by young people, who may themselves be recently converted, they will need wisdom and understanding of the particular issues involved in presenting Christ across cultural boundaries. Perhaps a shortened and simplified version of the Evangelical Alliance Commission's papers might help: and not only the children, but also grown-up English Christians, who have probably given little thought to the complexities that are involved.

Of course it is not a matter only of formal meetings, but of friendships, invitations to homes and sharing in social activities. Here, the evidence seems to be that in school and out the communities 'keep themselves to themselves'. Are they really Christian approaches if they do not lead to full and equal membership of God's family, which is reflected in hospitality on the human level?

In Conclusion

This essay is already over-long, but still no consideration has been given to the actual content, and little to the methods of 'Christian Approaches to People of Other Faiths in School'. Instead, an attempt has been made to survey the field, to ask questions and draw out some principles. For me, some basic principles were laid down long ago for William Carey's missionary community at Serampore:

> To refrain from whatever deepens India's prejudice against the Gospel.
> To esteem and treat Indians always as our equals.
> To acquaint ourselves with the snares which hold the minds of people (our minds as well as theirs).

These and others need to be drawn from the Word, deeply felt in the minds of those who would make Christian approaches, and adapted to the modern situation.

Many things about that situation are quite new. We used to talk of the 'foreign mission field', now about the 'mission field on our doorstep'. Then the target population was far away and colonial, if not alien; now we are talking of approaches to our next-door neighbours and our fellow-citizens. Then, missionaries learned a foreign language, now Asian children, if not their parents, speak English with the intonations and vocabulary of Birmingham or East-end London. Then missionaries were few, specialists and in a sense delegates, often working in rural areas; now all Christians are involved whether they realise it or not, and we live in an urban industrial society. Now we have television, an educative medium of great influence, which many Asian children watch for hours; then the medium was primarily the spoken word and the Book.

In both settings, schools have been seen and used as avenues for Christian approaches. In the overseas situation, mission schools have drawn out from a Muslim or Hindu population a relatively few young people, and education has been valued by them and their parents as a ladder of social mobility. Here all children go to school and for many children in inner city areas schools fulfil a different function. It is not really possible to assume that the models of overseas mission school will in fact be authentic guides in the in-Britain-now situation.

How then shall we proceed? By being realistic about what schools can and cannot do, what really are the outcomes of schooling for children of the 'immigrant' communities, and how this will affect their responses to Christian approaches. By recognising just how much our Christian approaches are compromised in the school situation and in society generally – and by repentance, restitution and reconciliation. By modelling our conduct on that of our Saviour: he became dependent upon the Samaritans when he stayed at Sychar overnight (John 4), so breaking contemporary conventions and taboos; he began where the woman of Sychar was, in her family situation and in her world-view, with her mountain as the centre of worship; he led her to understand that he was Messiah.

NOTES

1   M. Hobbs, *Teaching in a Multiracial Society*, London, Association of Christian Teachers, 1976.
2   See *Children and Race*, Milner, D, Penguin, 1975.

10

Practical Recommendations to the Church

D. L. E. BRONNERT AND R. W. F. WOOTTON

IN THIS CHAPTER WE SEEK TO EXAMINE DIRECTLY THE implications of the multi-faith society for the local church and to consider practical ways in which it should respond to the challenges and opportunities which this new situation affords. Many Christians who have lived long in a particular area are deeply troubled by the changes involved in the influx of people speaking a different language and having different customs from their own. They have perhaps been generous givers to Christian missions overseas, but it puzzles and confuses them when people from India or Africa move into the same street. Sometimes they may be influenced by other white people who talk about the 'problem of the immigrants' and resist the invasion of this 'alien element'. To see places given over to the worship of other faiths seems somehow to present a greater threat and troubles them more than the apostasy from Christianity of the great mass of people. But these are negative reactions; God calls us to positive responses to the situations which he has brought about. So let us think of God's call to his people today in multi-racial Britain and the opportunities he is creating for us. This applies not merely to those living in multi-racial areas or their immediate vicinity, but to all Christians everywhere.

1. Presence

The theology of Incarnation is no less fundamental for the Christian than that of the Atonement. Jesus came to live amongst those whom he died to save. The Christian always has to be identified closely with those to whom he is called to witness. The Christians of *these communities* are conspicuous more by their absence than their presence. Their Lord is calling his people to return to the back streets of our inner town multiracial communities to establish missionary churches. What is needed is a physical and psychological presence in the multi-racial area. It is obvious that degrees of involvement are likely; some will travel in to give valued occasional (or perhaps prolonged) assistance to churches in multi-racial areas, but the ideal remains, that of a literal, physical presence in a multi-racial area. More than physical presence is however needed, hence the reference to psychological presence – it is possible to live in one area and yet to have your children educated outside it, and for your thought-life and friendships to be in quite a different world. If the presence is to be real, it is to be a committed and involved presence in the local church life, and in the local community. Paternalistic and patronizing attitudes will of course obstruct; self-examination and repentance are essential, and all involvement must be out of a willingness to receive as well as a willingness to share and to give. If this policy is to become a practical reality there must be an attempt to inform Christians in all kinds of areas of the need in the multi-racial and industrial areas of Britain. It must be seen as the responsibility of the whole church, not just of the weak churches already in existence in multi-racial areas. Christian periodicals and Christian preachers have a responsibility in educating themselves and in helping to inform the Christian public the missionary needs of Britain. If Christians are to move, then they have to be housed and their children have to be educated, and they have to have spiritual and psychological support in the new and perhaps harsher environment they find themselves in. Some churches in multi-racial areas have seen the need for providing accomodation, and have involved themselves in housing associations and similar activities. As to education, many excellent schools exist in all kinds of areas: judgements need to be based on information rather than hearsay, and Christian conviction rather than social aspirations. Where a Christian's children attend local schools, this gives any number of opportunities of making friends, through walking to and fro with the children, attending functions at the school etc. As to spiritual and psychological support, there are existing churches providing a local nucleus of committed Christians. In some areas, a number of local churches seem likely to be closed, or have no vital spiritual life. God may lead Christians to such churches and such areas, but without a definite call, it would seem wiser to encourage Christians to move towards those churches where there is life and a future. Psychological and spiritual support is needed from Christians in the sending area as well as the receiving area; ordinary human links, visits, letters and phone calls, as well as continuing prayer support.

At the same time there is room too for Christians whose circumstances oblige them to live outside these areas, to be really involved with the people who live in them. This involvement will entail not only a real spiritual concern but also active interest in the social, economic and cultural life of the people of other faiths who live there. If we care for a person, we must care that he should be able to live his life with dignity; that he should not be humiliated; that he should be free to follow the manner of life he chooses; that his children should have fair opportunities in our society. This is a dimension of caring which evangelicals have sometimes tended to despise or neglect, but it is essential in this situation, for this is how we can show people how Christianity works in practical things (cf. Matt. 25, 31-46). So the Christian should be concerned for the community and aware of the problems of thee inner city where most immigrants live.

2. Preparation

Further, many white people, Christians included, are infected with racial prejudice; they have a feeling, often scarcely conscious, that coloured people are somehow inferior; they find it difficult to relate to them in a natural way, without being aloof or 'extra nice'. Clearly this is something the Christian must face frankly and repent of, if he finds himself after prayerful self-examination to be thinking in such a way. Many too are ethnocentric, i.e. they feel that British customs and culture are the norm and everything else is queer and eccentric. People forget that Indian civilisation antedates our own by thousands of years, and needs to be approached with humility and sensitivity. Before we can really draw close to our neighbour of another faith, we must know what his codes of behaviour, his values and basic assumptions about life and his attitude to us are likely to be. Without these we may easily offend unwittingly; we shall almost certainly find it impossible to communicate in any real sense. We also need to understand the special tensions placed upon our Hindu, Sikh, or Muslim neighbour by the society in which we all live: the problems of young people between two cultures, the problems of maintaining dietary rules, of preserving the family discipline and the standards of behaviour between the sexes which are part of their culture, and so on. We need not try to persuade ourselves that their way is necessarily the best, but we do need to have some insight into what it feels like to belong to an Asian community of faith in our secular society today.

3. Service

Jesus took the form of a servant. He said to the disciples, 'I am among you as one who serves'. He set us the example by washing the disciples' feet. If our presence as Christians within the community is to be truly evangelical and Christ-centred, we shall be known as the loving, serving, helping people of the community, to whom anyone can turn at any time. There are many areas of life where the Servant-Christ needs to be seen and heard, and as Christians we should seek to discover them and become involved. Service may be through the local church, or through a secular agency, or through an Asian community/religious agency. In undertaking any kind of service there needs to be research as to the real needs of the communities, and a genuine listening to the cries and opinions of the different groups in the community. 'We/they' attitudes must be avoided – the co-operation of others, especially in the group we wish to help, is essential. Among the obvious spheres of service in the secular community are children's play-groups, language teaching among Asians and advice centres. There are often needs for childminders and mothers' clubs. Where these already exist in the community, Christians need to be encouraged to participate with other people of

109

goodwill in such ventures. In one area an inter-faith group looks into local problems affecting all communities, such as traffic, litter etc; on one occasion it considered the needs of a particular Asian community, some of whose members were drifting into alcoholism, and the possibility of setting up an Alcoholics Anonymous group among them.

Where such social needs exist and no one is meeting them, the local church may well be instrumental in creating or stimulating such a response to human need. The ordinary life of the church in neighbourliness and service to the people in need ought to be a constant factor over and apart from any special activities. Involvement in Asian cultural activities and community programmes may occasionally present difficulties because of the religious implications involved. But there is no reason why Christians should not go as observers to places of other-faith worship, whether on ordinary occasions or at special festivals and celebrations. They must of course make it plain that they are interested and reverent *observers* and *not* worshippers, and refrain from any action, such as bowing before the sacred book or image, which, though meant simply as politeness, could be interpreted as actually joining in the worship. Asian friends are generally very happy to explain what is going on in English, so that language should not present a serious barrier. Supporting wherever possible what is good in the community and learning from those of a different culture and background is part of the Christian response. It contributes greatly to breaking down barriers and increasing mutual respect.

Another side of service in a multi-religious community is to engage in the debate about race and actively oppose the propaganda of racialist bodies such as the National Front and the National Party. In one city a few church leaders arranged a public meeting on the subject of 'Racial Justice Today', chaired by a Methodist minister and addressed by a bishop from southern Africa. The National Front was present in force and indulged in vociferous interruptions and abuse of the organisers and the coloured people present, so that it proved a very difficult meeting. But afterwards the comment was made that 'the Church has done what none of the political parties has dared to do – i.e. to hold a public meeting on the race issue'.

The exploitation of racial differences is not of course confined to the National Front and the National Party. At the other end of the political spectrum the Workers Revolutionary Party and similar groups will seize any opportunity to publicise their beliefs in confronting the political as well as the racial beliefs of their opponents. Local people who are members of other parties (even the British Communist Party) will sometimes prove valuable allies against both extremes.

Some may feel that this is too political an activity for church leaders to engage in, at least in any official capacity. But it should be remembered that the same argument was used by German churchmen in the thirties as an excuse for not opposing Hitler and denouncing his persecution of the Jews. There are times when men of God must take a clear stand on political issues in the name of righteousness, as did Amos, Jeremiah and others of the Hebrew prophets. Often people with strong political views but no Christian convictions show a much greater concern in this area than Christians, and so their belief that Christianity is irrelevant to the burning questions of the day is reinforced, and the people of other faiths learn to look for friendship and support elsewhere than among Christians. Some have argued that to speak on race issues only draws attention to the racialist organisations and gives them the publicity they want, but in fact, while many Christians have remained silent, these bodies have continued to grow in power and influence. Reluctance to take steps which may lead to controversy and unpleasantness and may prove unpopular even with some fellow-Christians who are influenced by racialism is natural, but it should not be disguised by specious arguments but rather faced and overcome. To take a stand on these issues will show our Asian friends that we really care for them as people and are prepared to back them, even at the cost of some personal unpopularity.

Another way in which Christians can serve the people of other faiths relates to the provision of buildings for their meetings and corporate activities of many kinds. In some areas there is a great shortage of public buildings, and the churches because of their long history are often the only private bodies with buildings which might be available. It is also true that some church halls are very much under-used, even in areas where there is a great shortage of halls. Secular activities, language classes, social and cultural gatherings etc., do not constitute a problem; on the contrary they are an avenue of service. Occasional use for wedding receptions falls in the same category and has often helped in establishing friendly links between the two communities concerned, but it should be noted that Hindu weddings normally take place in the same premises as the reception, and so people in charge of church halls may be giving permission for a religious ceremony without realising it. The whole question of the use of church buildings for religious teaching or worship in connection with another faith is a complex one, and is dealt with in a note at the end of this paper. (See p.000).

4. Dialogue

As Christians we need to keep open the lines of communication between ourselves and other people. This requires us to learn how to listen to other people and try to understand their thinking and where necessary their religious beliefs. This is not easy, it requires patience, understanding and love, plus a sensitivity to the Gospel. In practice it is often easier, and it seems more natural, to start what could be termed 'cultural dialogue' before getting involved in more personal and controversial religious dialogue. Sharing in the different ways of bringing up children and the different patterns of marriage are unthreatening ways of sharing in friendship, and Westerners may well feel that Eastern patterns of family life have much to teach us.

Before involving a Christian group in *religious* dialogue with those of another faith, it is essential that the group think beforehand about its own faith and have some basic knowledge of the other faith, so as to avoid feeling threatened or causing unnecessary offence to the other group. Christian groups always contain people of diverse Christian development and understanding – some, because their faith is somewhat uncertain and unformulated, may become belligerent, hostile and offensive when confronted with someone of another faith. Others, because they do not understand the differences between themselves and the other group, may concede vital

Christian truths in order to be friendly. All this underlines the need for thought and care before involving a Christian group in dialogue with people of another faith.

Some have suggested that the Christian and the other party in the dialogue should approach it with completely open minds, ready to be convinced by the other and to be converted to his faith. But for the person who has really come to know God 'in the face of Jesus Christ', this is not a possible option. At the same time he must be ready to listen with real attention, openness and honesty, to what the other person has to say and to welcome all that there is of truth and goodness which his friend has found. He may even be challenged in his own faith as he sees truths in it which he has not so far apprehended or perhaps has long ago forgotten. Thus as he hears a devout Muslim speak of the greatness of Allah, before whom he prostrates himself five times a day, with his forehead touching the ground as a symbol of his abasement before the majesty of his Creator, he may well recall that God is not simply the loving Father whom we can approach in wonderful intimacy – he is also the Sovereign Lord, the high and holy God who inhabits eternity. All truth is God's truth, and the Christian need have no fear of any truth that may meet him in another faith. After listening he will have the privilege of sharing the unfathomable riches of Christ in a gracious and humble way with the other person. Such an exercise is not itself preaching the gospel in the full sense but it may certainly have the effect of preparing the way for the Gospel, as well as giving the Christian a new insight into the other faith. Such occasions of dialogue may also be more formally structured, with speakers on a particular topic, such as 'knowing God', 'finding peace', 'the purpose of life', followed by open questions and then by discussion in small groups, perhaps with questions prepared beforehand; the last phase is generally the most profitable, as it involves personal meeting. It is best for Christians to engage in dialogue with one other faith at a time and not to involve themselves in a multi-faith exercise.

5. Proclamation

There are two dangers into which we often fall as Christians.

The first is to forget the importance of evangelism and witnessing. Many Christians become so absorbed in getting to know their Asian fellow-citizens, both as friends and as people with a particular, and often very fascinating, culture, outlook and religion, that they never go beyond to share with them the message of Jesus; or else perhaps they feel that to do so would be to put their new friendship at risk, forgetting that, if they truly love the other man, this itself carries with it the obligation of seeking to bring him into vital touch with Christ. The second danger is to rush into the preaching of the Gospel without the prior requirements of involvement, service and understanding. Neither is the way of Jesus. Our task is to preach Christ crucified, the Name above every name. It is encouraging to note that Bishop David Brown in his little book *A New Threshold* (BCC, 50p), while going much further than many Christians would in recognising the working of God in Islam, includes in his 'code of practice' for the churches: 'Christians ... have a continuing responsibility to share with all men the light and truth which has come to them through Christ, and to seek their freely-given allegiance to him'.

Jesus is the Saviour and Servant of all men – this is the message we must proclaim. Who does this? How is it to be done? What truths of the Gospel are particularly relevant? What are the cultural implications of the Gospel? Obviously evangelism is to be done by Christians, and the more it can be seen that British and Asian Christians are working together in the name of Christ, the more it will become plain that to be a Christian is distinct from being British. The Gospel is centred around the person of Jesus, and proclaiming the Gospel will mean proclaiming him positively. It is neither wise nor right to spend time attacking the cherished beliefs of others. Positively we need to commend Christ as the Saviour of all men. If the church is an oasis of ancient British culture or a celebration of a particular Anglo-Saxon highbrow intellectual group, then the possibility of winning others, whether Asian or working-class people, becomes very small. Yet the difficulties of trying to include different cultural groups in one fellowship are considerable; the situation is changing between the generations, and if the appeal is made to older cultural forms, whether British or Asian, then young people will quickly become disenchanted. Young Asian people are becoming less attached to their traditional culture as time goes on; the Asian convert to Christianity, because he is surrounded by British Christianity, is likely to become very British more rapidly. This would perhaps be deplorable in Asia, but is it so deplorable in Britain? An attempt to preserve the older Asian culture in the young convert may simply result in his failing to develop as a Christian. What matters is that both he and his British-born brethren in the church should realise that they all belong to the new community in Christ which challenges all culture and calls upon us to transcend it.

Methods of Evangelism

This is a subject on which much further study and experiment is needed, for precious little has been done so far, when one considers the millions of Christians in this country who pay lip-service at least to evangelism and the fact that many of the other-faith communities have been with us for about twenty years now. To some extent different methods may prove more fruitful with different communities – thus on the whole the Hindus are more literate than the others, and the Muslims more on the defensive. However in the following paragraphs we attempt to outline some of the principal methods which have been employed. In connection with all it is assumed that participants will approach the work in the spirit outlined in the earlier part of this chapter and after very careful preparation. This will involve not only an understanding of the culture and customs of the people approached (and these will vary somewhat between the different communities), but also some grasp of their religion and likely reactions to Christian evangelism. On the whole Asian people are much more ready to talk about religion than Westerners and to answer questions about their beliefs and practices; but they do of course resent any slur on their own beliefs, whether direct or implied. In addition to material in this book, tapes are available from the Bible and Medical Missionary Fellowship (352 Kennington Rd, London S.E.11), and the Lutterworth Press's 'Christian Approach' series about the various faiths will prove helpful in this aspect of preparation.

115

(a) *A mission of friendship*. This is really a matter rather of pre-evangelism than of evangelism proper. It consists in planned visits by a local church or several churches working together to the Asian homes in the area in order to express a friendly attitude, a desire to get to know the people visited and a willingness to help in practical ways if there should be any particular need, e.g. to help in filling up forms for a government office or to teach someone English. A specially prepared leaflet in English and the appropriate Asian languages with the addresses and telephone numbers of church officers etc., can be left in each home. At this stage it is suggested that no directly religious approach should be made but that the emphasis should be on friendship and helping. Asian homes can generally be recognised by the names entered in the electoral role, which is available for study in the chief public libraries.

It is good to go together in pairs, but it is preferable that people of different sexes should not be teamed up together unless they are man and wife or brother and sister; otherwise there is a possibility of misunderstanding, except in the most Westernised homes.

(b) *A Gospel distribution campaign*. In a number of places such campaigns have been carried out through the efforts of inter-church committees and volunteers. The Bible Society is prepared to supply Gospels in English (Good News Bible version) and the Asian languages at a greatly reduced rate for free distribution. The diglot gospels of Luke in English with Urdu, Panjabi or Gujarati are specially effective. Sometimes a loose cover is added with an appropriate title, such as 'Good News for All', and an address or addresses where those interested are invited to make further inquiries, though in fact few people respond to this invitation. Each gospel is given personally and only to those who say they are interested to read it. Where people seem especially interested (though sometimes this is just politeness) a further visit can be made later. To distribute gospels to the whole population in this way and not just to the Asians high-lights the universality of the Gospel. In one town it was possible to engage practically all the churches in such a campaign, because it was done for the whole community. This meant praying together and sharing common concerns, and involved Asian and English Christians visiting, together with West Indian Christians as well. Sharing thus in a common task brought down any number of barriers and suspicions.

(c) *A visitation campaign*. Sometimes churches have undertaken the systematic visitation of an area, not simply to offer gospels but to engage people directly in conversation about their attitude to Christ and the Christian message. This may take the form of a long-term programme rather than a short campaign. The Christian workers take with them gospels and other Christian literature, often for sale rather than free distribution. This kind of campaign, unless handled with real sensitivity, can be counter-productive, as Asian people are quick to resent an aggressive kind of evangelism. Many of them feel threatened in view of the racialist propaganda met with in many places – offensive slogans scrawled on walls etc. – and evangelism of this kind may seem a threat to their own ways and their family life, for even in this country it is difficult for someone converted to Christ to remain within a family that professes another faith.

(d) *Evangelistic meetings*. Though sometimes Asian people will drop into church services largely out of curiosity, it is not easy to get them along to meetings in church premises. This can sometimes be arranged as a return when a Christian group has already visited a temple, and it can be partly a social occasion with refreshments (here care must be taken about food taboos). Sometimes people who have been visited and seem to show some interest can be invited to a meeting on neutral ground (a community centre, for instance); this may take the form of a talk followed by discussion or a Christian film or play. At such meetings Indian music, live if possible, will be an attraction; there are Punjabi Christian choirs in some areas. Pressure for immediate decisions is not recommended, for any response may prove superficial.

(e) *Children's work*. Up to the age of about 12 Asian parents will sometimes allow their children to join Scouts, Guides, Boys Brigade, Covenanters or similar organisations, partly no doubt with the idea that this will help them in speaking English and in social mixing. Successful Bible Clubs have been run in some places. The children will often absorb Christian teaching in this way, like the Sikh girl who was asked how

117

when she thought of God she pictured him, and answered at once, 'Like Jesus'. But they should not at this age be put into a position of conflict with their families. On rare occasions Asian parents of other faiths have allowed their children in such circumstances to be baptised and join a church; this may be more common in the future, as the hold of the traditional faiths is bound to be relaxed somewhat (for better or for worse) in secular Britain, and opportunities of evangelism among the youngsters of Asian homes will grow.

(f) *Young people's work.* Often parents withdraw their children from scouts, Sunday School etc., at the age of 12 and insist on their receiving instruction in their own religion. Even so some Christians have managed to run recreation clubs, Bible Study groups etc., in the evenings, at weekends or even during the school lunch break. Normally separate arrangements must be made for teenage boys and girls, as parents will not wish them to mix, and girls may have to be collected from their homes, as parents may not allow them out on their own, especially at night. Occasionally mixed camps have been run at centres in the country under careful supervision, with food taboos observed. Young people, when ready for it, may be invited to commit their lives to Christ, but they must know what it may cost. Much wisdom and tact will be needed to cope with problems which will arise at their homes, whether they receive baptism or not – this cannot of course take place till they are 18, except with their parents' consent.

(g) *Literature distribution.* The majority of the Asian adults can read one or more of the five languages, Gujarati, Panjabi, Urdu, Bengali and Hindi. Few other books in these languages are obtainable in this country (though public libraries carry stocks), so attractive Christian literature is often acceptable. As well as the Bible Society and the Scripture Gift Mission (for Scripture selections) the Christian Literature Crusade is the main supplier. The ideal arrangement for distribution is a Christian bookshop, where people can come in not only to buy books in English and Asian languages but also to converse with the staff about the things they have read. In addition, gospels have even been sold to the crowds leaving or entering one of the many Indian cinemas of Britain's multi-racial areas.

Note I – Inter-faith Worship

Many Christians today feel it is right to adopt a generally positive attitude to other faiths, that is, to appreciate all that is good and true in them and to place emphasis on this rather than on any negative aspects. Some would carry this attitude to the point of joining in worship with people of other faiths, and public services of this kind take place from time to time, in which scriptures of the other different faiths are read and prayers are said according to their varying practices; on some occasions solemn theological affirmations are also made together. It is plausibly argued that by so doing Christians acknowledge the working of God in other faiths, strengthen the ties of mutual understanding and respect and at the same time bear witness with others to a supernatural life in a world of materialism and unbelief.

Such an attitude raises a number of problems:

1. How far can such worship be meaningful when the whole concept of God is radically different, as between the great monotheistic faiths, Buddhist agnosticism and Hindu monism (i.e. the concept of the unity of all existence without the distinction between Creator and Creation)?

2. What would be its effect on new Christians converted from the other faiths and any who are weak in faith?

3. Is it compatible with the evangelism which Christ commanded as a primary duty of his church?

4. Does this imply a recognition of the equality of all religions as equally valid ways to God?

While all these points are important, the last raises the key issue. Some professing Christians frankly accept such equality between the great world religions, but this position contradicts the faith of the Scriptures and of the Church. Someone has said, 'Christ is either Lord of all or not Lord at all', and St Peter boldly affirmed that he is indeed Lord of all, though at the same time recognising that God-fearing men of every nation are acceptable to God (Acts 10:34–36). Clearly then inter-faith worship is unacceptable when it implies such a recognition of other faiths.

But does this rule out inter-faith worship altogether? There are many occasions where something which might be termed inter-faith worship is fully compatible with Christian loyalty. Thus members of different faiths have sometimes engaged in worship successively in the presence of each other, each observing rather than participating in the other groups' worship. Again, people of different faiths have listened together to readings from the various scriptures and then made affirmations of a moral and social (but not theological) character; for instance resolutions to work for mutual understanding and tolerance, to resist racialism and discrimination etc. Again, people engaged in a dialogue conference, who have reached a level of personal rapport and clearly understand each other's position, have sometimes felt able to join together in intercession for deeply felt needs without compromising their loyalty to their own faith.

Sometimes too special circumstances arise, as when on an occasion of mourning for a young Sikh killed in a brawl by white youths, Christian ministers felt it was clearly right for them to engage in prayer in the presence of the Sikh mourners.

These are just a few of the possible situations where a Christian can engage with a good conscience in something approaching inter-faith worship, indeed perhaps ought to do so. But these do not contradict the main thesis that when inter-faith worship involves an implicit denial of the basic claims of Christ it is clearly inadmissible. As the British Council of Churches resolved in 1968: 'Churches should scrupulously avoid those forms of inter-faith worship which compromise the distinctive faiths of the participants and ensure that Christian witness is neither distorted nor muted'.

Note II – The Use of Church Buildings

If the Church wishes to serve the whole community in the name of Christ, it will be happy to have its buildings used for social, cultural and similar purposes by people of other faiths. The problem arises about their *religious* use, whether for worship or for teaching young people, as in the Quranic schools found in many of our cities.

Few would disagree with the conclusion of the British

Council of Churches Working Party, reporting on this subject in 1974, that 'buildings devoted to regular Christian worship should not be made available for the acts of worship of other faiths'. In fact such use is rarely, if ever, requested; but if it were granted it would clearly lead to great confusion in the minds of Christians and of the community at large.

The real issue concerns church halls, school rooms and other auxiliary buildings. Here the BCC Working Party recommended: 'Those who can do so conscientiously, legally and with pastoral responsibility should also make such premises available to people of other Faiths for their religious purposes.' At the same time they envisaged two exceptions – 'groups indulging in derogatory misrepresentations of the Christian Faith for propaganda purposes, and those intending to practise on the premises grosser forms of worship'. Another possible exception would be those groups which definitely seek to win converts from the native community, like the Divine Light Mission and the Hari Krishna movement; in theory all Muslims should fall in this category, but in practice they do not.

The attitude underlying the desire to offer hospitality is no doubt based on the principle of Lev. 19:34: 'You shall love the alien as yourself', and perhaps also on the conviction that people of other faiths should not only be given full freedom in the practice of their faith but should even be actively encouraged to do so, as this enables them to keep a sense of identity and saves them from the ever-present danger of lapsing into secularism. It is argued that a church may with a good conscience express its hospitality in this way and at the same time make its own position plain, confirming its claims by active commitment to evangelism and using the closer links to which the loan of a building should lead as an opportunity to make Christ known.

Others however feel that to sanction such use of church buildings is bound to give the impression that Christians are acknowledging the other faiths as fully valid for their adherents and that thereby they are compromising the absolute claims of Christ and in effect renouncing any evangelistic aims. In this view (which the present writers do not share) such a policy greatly strengthens the other-faith community in its religious life and thus makes it more difficult to approach people with the Christian message. Further, if any from the group in question have turned to Christ, their minds are confused and their faith weakened by seeing what appears to be an alliance between their new faith and the one that they have left at great personal sacrifice.

Another question concerns church buildings which are no longer needed for their original purpose. If the Christian commitment to freedom of worship and assembly is to be given positive expression, there needs to be a willingness to consider selling redundant sites and buildings, and positively to assist those who wish to find places for worship. It is felt by many Christians that to sell to a non-Christian group is an admission of the failure of the Gospel; it is plain for all to see that what was once a Christian centre has now been handed over as a mosque or temple. It should be no part of a Christian's life or the churches' practice to disguise the reality. If Christians have moved from the area, or if local people have abandoned the worship of Christ, it is difficult to justify retaining an empty shell; for 'the most high God does not live in houses built by men' (Acts 7:48). In quite a number of areas this issue is largely a thing of the past; groups now seeking buildings can in many cases be splinter groups from existing temples etc. The principle of freedom of worship and assembly does not of course mean the promotion of fragmentation in religious groups.

Part Three

They Speak for Themselves

11

What has Buddhism brought to the West?

CHRISTMAS HUMPHREYS

IN NOVEMBER 1974 THE BUDDHIST SOCIETY COMPLETED THE first fifty years of its work in Britain. This paper is a consideration of what it has offered the West and with what success.

The inquiry involves three factors: the strangeness of ideas imported; the conditions of Western thought at the time and in the years following; and how the ideas have been presented and to what effect.

We, the Buddhist Society, were not first in the field. The Pali Text Society, founded by the Rhys Davids in 1881, had made the Pali Canon available in English to scholars; the Theosophical Society had given a wide circle of enquirers far more of the esoteric Buddhism of Tibet than has yet appeared in current literature, together with a complete outline of cosmo- and anthropogenesis, and something of the Wisdom-religion which has been called the 'accumulated wisdom of the ages'; and the Buddhist Society of Great Britain and Ireland, founded in 1907 to receive the English bhikku Ananda Metteyya, had explained in public lectures the basic principles of Theravada Buddhism.

But these were alien ideas indeed which the new Buddhist movement offered the Western enquirer, in the face of dogmatic theology, grossly material science and a sadly materialistic analysis of the working of the mind. Tolerance of every different religion – a preposterous idea!; the cosmic law of Karma/Rebirth as a substitute for a personal yet Almighty God; an individual yet interdependent Way of life to a clearly defined spiritual goal; the existence of the 'Buddha-Mind' or Spirit or the 'god within' already fully existing in every individual's mind, yet without a separate immortal soul; the Bodhisattva ideal of limitless compassion for all forms of life, born of an awareness that Life is one; the limits of the power of the intellect versus the exclusive ability of the intuition to know Truth as such; and Nirvana as a spiritual goal beyond description existing here and now. All this in addition to the Nobel Eightfold Path to the end of suffering for every man and all mankind. Save for a few scholars and members of the Theosophical Society, these principles were *new*!

New to the whole range of Western thought with its heavy load of conditioning. The Christian background of every European could not be shrugged off, even by the foolish who chose to ignore the strength and beauty of the teachings of the man Jesus. But Christianity as a force was dying, stricken by its inability to prevent or even explain a fractricidal war between a dozen so-called Christian countries. This left a gap to be filled, a spiritual void, and neither science nor psychology, nor any of the 'isms' of the day could fill it. And not even Buddh–ism we realised would fill it straight away. There was need of new life, not ancient forms, of some new splendour of awareness which would lift the mind beyond the psychic plane of spiritualism, beyond the moral plane of ethics, beyond noble concepts of high-thinking philosophers, beyond any ritual or mass-emotion of religious revival. Some force, some vision, was needed of a far Beyond, beyond all definition yet clearly perceived as a light already within. Such we believed was the Buddha-Dharma, at its noblest, widest, highest, most illuminated best.

Its strength, we believed, was this, that it was not merely the Wisdom acquired by one man, whom H. G. Wells, in no sense a religious man, described as the greatest man that ever lived. Even the Buddha, in his last incarnation, only taught a portion of the Ancient Wisdom which is the common heritage of the human mind. Man is very old, say the Hindus, and a full cycle of his coming-to-be and his ceasing-to-be is a figure of 311,040 and nine noughts, not to be laughed off in our present knowledge of light years. He has slowly learned from experience, and taught what he has learned, and there are those, the Teachers, Masters, Rishis, Mahatmas, Roshis and noble lamas, who are guardians of this Wisdom and teach it, in form and place, as men have need of it. All religions have been and will be part of it, and from it any gap in a nation's or people's mind will be filled.

And so to our times. In 1875 two Masters of the Wisdom in Tibet sent H. P. Blavatsky, their pupil, to the West to meet Col. H. S. Olcott in the U.S.A. and to re-form the Theosophical movement. An editor of an Indian newspaper, A. P. Sinnet, was put in touch with these Masters and a correspondence ensued over four years. These letters, now in the British Museum, were published early in 1924 as the *Mahatma Letters to A. P. Sinnet*. From them Sinnet wrote *Esoteric Buddhism*, and from her training H. P. Blavatsky wrote *The Secret Doctrine*, in which a great deal of esoteric Buddhism is given us by a woman who regarded the Buddha as the Master of Masters, the supreme teacher of this age. In 1891 she died, and in 1906 Col. Olcott died. In 1908 Ananda Metteyya, an English bhikku, arrived in London and for the first time presented an English audience with Buddhism as a way for the English man and woman to follow – practical Buddhism, Buddhism applied. Sinnet died in 1921 – I was just able to correspond with him – and at about the same time the old Society petered out with the death of its founders. This present Society founded in 1924, was composed of the remnants of the old Society, members of the Theosophical Society, and a few more, and for fifty years, we have tried too fill that gap with teachings of the Ancient Wisdom, which in the West, as in the East, are appropriate for any hungry mind. The Societies' methods for 'publishing and making known the fundamental principles of Buddhism' have been wide and various, including lectures, classes, meditation, the Middle Way and books and pamphlets, its Correspondence Course and Summer School, its affiliated groups throughout the country and its close connection with the Viharas and other Buddhist societies as they come and go. What in these fifty years have we offered the West of Buddhist principles, effective in the minds of thousands to show them the Way to the end of suffering, to heart's peace, and the opening phases of enlightenment?

I must confine myself to seven. First, *Toleran e*, in 1924 presenting in London a tradition unique in the history of religion. Never in 2,500 years of Buddhism has a man's hand been lifted against a fellow man for a different opinion as to the Buddha- Dharma, and in Nalanda, the great University of the East, for nine hundred years a thousand teachers taught ten thousand pupils all that was known of the Buddha's teaching, and, so visitors tell us, in perfect harmony of learning. Where Buddhism has reached a new country there was teaching and example, not the sword, and indigenous religions were, if willing, gently assimilated. Today the World Fellowship of Buddhists is witness to the communion of its many schools.

Secondly, *Karma and Rebirth*, the twin doctrines with which Buddhists replace the concept of an Almighty yet Personal God. In Buddhism the manifested universe is absolute harmony, and he who breaks it mends it, at the cost of suffering. Whether viewed at cosmic, metaphysical level, as the casual interdependence of every movement of the Life-force in all aspects of its operation, or, as in the Therevada school, as at least the inescapable law of moral retribution – 'we are punished *by* our sins not for them' – all that we know is Law-begotten, and every motion of the Life-force in any human mind bears fruit in every corner of the vast field of our becoming. The Law is as old as man, and older still, for it made him what he is. And Rebirth is, in classic Buddhist teaching, the inevitable corollary. We sleep each night and wake to another day's work, bearing the consequences of unexpended causes during the day before. So we die to a longer sleep, and wake to a further stage on the long road to perfection. It is not surprising that thousands in the West prefer this doctrine, a matter of experience for all who check its working, to the vague, unjust alternative of chance, or the will of an extra-cosmic God.

Thirdly, we have stressed to the West the *Middle Way*, and an Eightfold Path which treads it carefully. It lies between all extremes, for all extremes are wrong, between the intellectual creations of dialectic and science on the one hand, and emotionalism and personality-worship on the other, between 'heart' and 'head'. Above both shines the flame of the intuition, by which alone all opposites are seen in synthesis, and the Western tension of science versus theology, thought versus feeling, and for that matter, East versus West, are viewed from the totality of which they are twin semblances in manifestation.

Do we see in current Western life some better awareness of this principle, a symbiosis of 'get together' of man and master, science and religion, and both 'right'? At least this Middle Way is a straight road, needing no apparatus for its treading, beneath our feet each moment of the day.

Fourthly a new (for the West) *relationship for the individual and the whole*, whether the whole be the collective job, the Borough Council or the Government of the day. The individual has its rights against oppression and anarchy, in favour of freedom under law. But he has his duties too within the Dharma – a term which covers duty, natural law, spiritual teaching – which the Buddha proclaimed as existing for all to see. As he has his rights in respect of his fellow men, each and all of them, so he has his duty to each and all. Here is 'interdependent independence', freedom, but the only possible freedom, freedom within the law. On the one hand there is the discipline of the law of the land and the moral law; on the other the self-discipline which alone can give the whole stability.

Fifthly, the tremendous spiritual principle, surely self-evident to any probing mind, that *Life is one*. The Life-force in every living thing – and there is nothing dead – is the same life, and its forms are therefore brothers. Hence compassion, the driving awareness of impersonal love for all that suffer, all in need, and that means all mankind. This Bodhisattva doctrine of Mahayana Buddhism is one of the greatest contributions of Buddhism to world religion; here is the feeling of the heart combined with the wisdom of the head, and a faculty developed which combines and is the source of both. Are there faint stirrings of this cosmic love today in the bizarre and socially destructive habits of a section of youth in all parts of Europe? They destroy tradition as such, break laws as such, but as yet have no constructive alternative. But is there stirring here a sense that life is one and its individual manifestations are one, and that each is in some sense as good as another, with rights as such but with duties as yet unperceived?

Sixthly, there is a rising warfare in the West on *the ambit of the intellect*. The intellect knows more and more *about*; it can never *know*. This is the function of the intuition, the light of the Spirit, or Buddha-mind within, which, as more and more perceived and trusted, illumines the field of thought and turns mere concept into certainty. It is interesting to note that more and more scientists admit that the greatest discoveries come not with thought, but when thought as such has been for the moment transcended. Here is Wisdom, the Beauty beyond all forms of it, Compassion as spiritual strength which flows into each opportunity. It is as far beyond that as thinking is beyond physical sensation. This is 'knowing beyond formulation', a periodic breakthrough to pure Truth.

And seventhly, in this brief choosing, Buddhism has taught, as every Eastern religion has ever taught, *a Beyond, achievable here and now*. It is indeed both here and now, the Spirit in the flesh, the God within the animal, which, as a growing unit of life, is man. We find it in the experience of intuitive flashes, the reward of thinking beyond thought to the limit of our own already possessed enlightenment. To the Buddhist, Nirvana is total absorption in full awareness into an existence without a sense of separate self. It is the goal of infinite effort, made life after life on earth to the end of a Path whose opening steps are here and now.

Meditation is a means to spiritual progress in use in the East from time immemorial and now, in forms both sound and evil, appearing as a new interest – one hopes more than a passing craze – in the West. Only sound teachers, right motive and common sense will distinguish the helpful from evil practices which lead, in frightening numbers to insanity.

These principles we have taught, and more. Have we succeeded in our object, 'to publish and make known the principles of Buddhism'? The answer appears to be yes, for in fifty years we have published literature in many forms, stimulated the publication of endless books on Buddhism, sent lecturers far and wide, assisted in the formation of provincial Buddhist groups, and in other ways taught 'suffering and the end of suffering', which the Buddha stated to be the essence of his message to mankind.

At least the genesis of Buddhism, and something of it schools and terms are known to the reading public, and this spread of interest cannot be unconnected with the growing demand for the theory and practice of religion of every kind. Scores of colleges and schools now ask for information for their courses in comparative religion, of which Buddhism appears to be the most popular. We hear and see Buddhism described on radio and television in a way unthinkable twenty years ago. The Dharma, it seems, is here to stay.

But have we succeeded in the second half of our object, 'to encourage the study and application of Buddhist principles'? Judging by the interest roused, our membership, the size of the reading public, and the confirmation of Buddhist principles, often openly, by science, psychology, and in the field of sociology, the answer again is yes. We have shown the Buddha's way to enlightenment without warring politics or murderous, competitive egotism, without the necessity of ritual or the least use of drugs. Here are principles which no degeneration based on fear can reduce or water down. Here is a truer view on the nature of self and Self, as long ago made clear in the Dhammapada.

At least all educated men and women know of Buddhism, and thousands some of its principles. It is for the individual to study and then tread the way, and to tread it happily with ceaseless effort and the light of joy, to the end which many are fast approaching and some, it would seem, have already reached. These are indeed Buddhists. And the rest of us? Why burden ourselves with a label? What matters is the man within, his strength of purpose, his vision of the Goal, his full compassion for all forms of the One Life. These will lead him to enlightenment, and when the majority of mankind or at least concerned with such a Way there will be peace on earth but not before. And the formula for success? In the Buddha's dying words: 'Strive mightily'.

12

Hinduism in Britain

VISHNU NARAYAN

FOR SOME STRANGE REASON, WESTERN PEOPLE HAVE suddenly become aware of India, and the Indian influence is increasingly emerging as a very strong force in Western history. But the discovery of India is still going on.

One day, back in 1967, after I had given a talk on Aurobindo to a gathering of English people, I was approached at the end of the meeting by an elderly English gentleman who, by chance, had served in the Indian Army, 'Pandit Narayan', he said, 'could I make a cynical observation?' 'By all means', I replied. 'Well', he went on, 'it seems that we went to India and conquered it. We ruled over it but never cared for the values it had to give us. Now it seems, we realise how foolish we were, because every other person is closing his eyes, and doing meditation.'

On another occasion, in 1967, I went to Rolle College, Exmouth, to give a talk on Hinduism, and after the lecture, the Head of Divinity told me: 'I am glad now that the people of India have come to this country, because now I feel that the encounter with Indians, and especially with Hindus, will deepen the Christian experience.' At last we are beginning to realise how important it is for a person to come into contact with other cultures, if he really wants to understand himself, and I must say, that for my part, standing face to face with other cultures has proved to be a kind of mirror to me, and has widened and deepened my own religious experience.

After coming to this country, Hindus have become very conscious of their heritage and culture, although of course they are very religious by nature. Technology has, as it were, brought all the religions into the 'melting pot', and Hinduism is no exception. I think in many respects, Indian and British societies are strikingly similar. Since the dawn of history, a great experiment has been going on in India, as to how people of different races, culture and belief can live together in peace and harmony, and now the same thing is happening here in Britain. I would say, that on the whole, the average British person is very tolerant towards people of other faiths. Initiatives have been taken to 'break the ice' and understand each other, and the encounters between the different religious persuasions in Britain have produced a unique situation.

I have had the opportunity of attending conferences and seminars, where priests and adherents of different religious denominations have expressed their views with complete understanding and sympathy with each other. Fifty years ago, this would not have been possible. In the 1960s I was working with Burns & Oates, the Catholic firm of publishers, and I was especially interested in their attitude and that of the Vatican, after Pope John XXIII made his statement that although Christ is the fulfilment of all religions, yet there is truth in all religions and we must be patient and learn from each other.

During the last decade our population has increased tremendously, and there has been a great Hindu upsurge. Religious organisations have sprung up, and empty churches have been bought often with great difficulty, and have been converted into Temples. Each year, we try to celebrate our religious and cultural festivals, even if we cannot quite create the same atmosphere as we enjoyed in India. Weddings, funerals and other sacraments are performed as they would have been in our homeland, but in a modified way, and Hindus have learned to preserve their values and cultural traditions even in a highly organised society such as we have in Britain, where things move at a tremendous pace.

A wedding in India, conducted with the colouring of family customs and provincial ritual, can take four or five hours to perform, and the feasting and gaiety which follows can last for days and days, and nights and nights. In England, the wedding ceremony usually lasts about an hour and a half, and including the feasting, the entire proceedings will only last four or five hours. The rituals are modified, and only the necessary parts of them are performed. Sometimes the priest will translate the rituals into English, for the benefit of those younger people who have been born in England and who have not learned their native tongue.

It has been the custom of Hindus in Britain to hire a hall from the local authority to celebrate weddings, and unfortunately some civic authorities are now refusing to let us have the use of their halls, as there have been complaints that the floors have been damaged during the lighting of the sacrificial fire. In the *Sunday Mirror* once I read an article asking 'whether Hindu love was not too hot to handle', and a mock marriage was formed to see whether the fire which was kindled could be easily controlled. Nowadays we take extra precautions to see that great care is exercised during the lighting of the sacrificial fire, and that the floor and surrounding area is very well protected. Most marriages in India take place in the open air, under a canopy, but due to the climate this is just not possible in Britain. At a Hindu wedding, usually around two hundred people are present, but sometimes up to a thousand guests are entertained, and we do need community halls, 'a place of our own', where weddings and festivals can be conducted.

Our weddings are performed to the accompaniment of Shahanai music, and this tends to give the impression to English people that a Hindu wedding is purely a secular occasion. This is, incidentally, another reason why local authorities refuse to let us have the use of their halls on Sundays. However, it is an incorrect assumption, and our Shahanai music is equivalent to the organ and choir which is the traditional accompaniment to a Christian wedding.

As far as funerals are concerned we have more or less accepted the British tradition (do we have any option?), and I think it is right to follow the custom of the host country, if possible, without our ceremony losing its religious significance. In most cases, priests go to houses where the mourners are gathered to perform a few rituals, and from there to the crematorium. I have asked one crematorium if we would be allowed to use our 'Om' symbol, instead of the cross, during the time of the funeral service, and this has been granted. We never really minded the cross symbol being used, because we do not purposely disrespect any religious symbol, but the

'Om' sign is more meaningful to us.

It is very interesting to observe how, without any institutionalised or organized effort, Indian culture has penetrated into the West – in the form of Yoga, Krishna-consciousness, Vedanta, Tantra, and so on. It has not come into the West because it was imported from the East, but rather because Western society itself is eager to experiment and see whether there is anything worthwhile in it.

In 1964, I went to give a talk to a church in Mill Hill, and afterwards a devout Christian told me that 'we feel guilty if we close our eyes for a few minutes and do nothing, because we have been trained not to waste time'. Now it seems that the trend has been reversed. We read everywhere that we should take things easy, meditate, discover the Kingdom of Heaven within.

The spiritual genius of Hinduism 'governs all life; it fills all thought; it governs all acts; it regulates all movements. In this unique and most atmospheric quality lies the haunting power of India – and even those Westerners who have no contact with its actual source are subtly affected, and sometimes haunted for the rest of their lives, by that in India which they cannot name.' (*Catholic Encounter with World Religions*, H. Van Straelen, Burns and Oates).

Now it is up to the British people to see if this statement is true, for certainly India's spiritual culture has never received so much attention from the West as in the last few years. And not only is it the spiritual culture which is under scrutiny – Indian curry is now the third most popular dish on the British menu, and the disciplines of Hatha Yoga are being undertaken daily by more and more people. Although Hatha Yoga is approached initially as a 'body cult', it soon leads the aspirant to a sincere adherence to Indian spiritual beliefs. In the country of 'Amen' the great syllable 'Om' is now beginning to vibrate throughout the land.

Yet a great deal of concern is being expressed by our social thinkers, that in fifteen years' time there will not be a sufficient number of priests among the Hindu community in England to carry on the religious work, and if great care is not taken now to educate those children who have been born here then they may forget their spiritual heritage and lose their sense of identity. Not enough is being done to educate our children, who are the future 'lights' of Hinduism, and soon only a miracle will save our community from this disaster. Yet our culture has been under attack before. In our native India we were overcome by oppressors, temples were destroyed, and the people were enslaved for hundreds of years, and yet we had the tenacity to keep the culture alive, and live the spiritual values meaningfully. Can we do the same thing again? Can we keep our culture and our spiritual values in the face of materialism and the restless pace of Western technology? I firmly believe that we can. And yet I feel that perhaps our values will survive in a new form, with a fresh outlook, but that the lustre of the Divine will shine through them. 'The outstanding literary, philosophic and scientific genius of almost all countries have more or less got this spirit of the vedantic conception of life, and have jealously been upholding this principle as the panacea for all the corroding ills the modern world is subject to.' 'Since the beginning of spiritual awakening Hindus have constantly tried to fathom the mystery of the Divine, through the inexhaustible abundance of myths, philosophy, or one or another kind of Yoga such as Gnana, Bhakti, or Karma, using the Law of Karma and the transmigration of souls as a wayfarer, to come to the state of consciousness as a witness, of consciousness freed from its psycho-physiological structures and their temporal conditioning, the consciousness of the liberated man, of him who has succeeded in emancipating himself from temporality, and therefore knows the true inexpressible freedom. The quest of this absolute freedom, of perfect spontaneity, is the goal of all Indian philosophies and mystical techniques, but it is above all through one of the many forms of Yoga that India has held that it can be assured' (Renoir, *La Polytheisme Hindeau*).

Hinduism is a way of life and a religious tradition of the Indian people as such which is 'not opposed to any faith, any prophet, any incarnation, or any method of spiritual realisation, since one of its basic principles is to make a place within itself for them, and for all forms of religious experience of the past, and of the future. The eternal law of Perfection teaches us that every belief in every age is given the forms of revelation which it requires, and that within these forms or outside them, each individual must discover for himself, in accordance with his state of development, a distinct road to realisation, and the forms of prayer which meet his needs, the morality, the rites, and the gods, which are his own. The task of the spiritually awakened man, the person who possesses a fragment of the truth, is simply to pass on to qualified novices those things which he himself has experienced, and nothing else. He cannot claim that he possesses the only truth, for he cannot know what appears true in the eyes of others' (*Yoga, Immortality and Freedom*, Mircea Eliade).

Wherever we Hindus have come to live, we always try to live in peace and harmony. We never tend to impose our views or religions on others for we do not believe in converting others to our religion. If I may quote the Bhagavad Gita: 'In any way that men love me, in that same way they find my love, for many are the paths of men, but they all in the end come to me' (Bhag. Gita Ch.4:11).

Even so, we can be misunderstood and misinterpreted; perhaps we ourselves are partly responsible for this, but I believe that through the exchange of ideas, and through spreading the knowledge of our customs and beliefs, we have a great deal to contribute to British society in helping to establish peace and harmony. We also, in our turn, have much to learn from the British society, and I sometimes wish that we could be more organised.

What about our domestic scene? By and large, on the surface there is no difference between a Hindu home and that of a westerner. The kitchen, living room, sitting room and so on, are the same in both, as is the cooker, the crockery and the cutlery. However, there are subtle differences. In the Hindu home, the mother will make curry and chapattis, and in one corner of the house one would invariably find a murti of either Ganesh, Shiva, Durga, Rama or Krishna, or even Buddha or Christ, in front of which, each day, after taking her bath, the housewife will burn a candle and a joss stick, and place there some flowers and food, and seek a blessing for the day from the deity. In most houses we continue to observe our family prayers, but some families experience difficulties and say that, due to the influence of television, it is extremely difficult for them to educate their children in a religious way; after all, they are living in the British society. It would be helpful if there could be more programmes on television geared to the immigrant community – twenty-five minutes on Sunday morning is really not long enough, and we would like to see programmes depicting the Mahabharata or the Ramayana.

We do try to observe our various festivals in a limited way, even if we cannot have the pleasure of splashing coloured water on the day of 'Holi' festival, or of lighting the many candles on 'Deevali' day, or of observing the 'Durga Puja' as it is celebrated in Bengal for ten days. Sometimes, when we are observing a festival, the unnatural atmosphere gives one the feeling that we are not really celebrating it at all, we are just making a mock of it simply to convince ourselves, but given time, perhaps a sense of homeliness will emerge. At the moment, though, we are still the newcomers. Would that we would recapture the same kind of religious conviction that the Christians felt the first century after Christ, or when the Jewish people were persecuted and came to settle in India. Even today, you can see a Jewish woman in India, clad in saris, and looking no different to Indian women, yet they are Jewish and observe the Jewish festivals, and the Parsees are still Persians in India, kindling their fires and performing their rituals.

I recently read in a sociological magazine 'New Society' that Indian children are generally better behaved than their English school mates, that they are less violent and more interested in doing well in their school work and availing themselves of the opportunities provided in the British educational system. Could this be because they are contented at home? Hindu children are taught to respect their mother, father, teacher and guest, and this great precept, taught by Hindu sages, still holds true in most Hindu homes, and the sense of respect towards their elders does not necessarily suppress the children's personality growth. Here again, I have heard some families express concern that they are finding it difficult to command the children's respect, often again because of the influence of television.

At the moment I give lectures on behalf of the London University Extra-Mural Dept., on Indian Culture and Sanskrit, and in that class of twenty-three students, sixteen of them are British. I wonder why they want to learn Sanskrit and Indian culture?

Some time ago I was interviewed in the ITV programme 'Believe it or Not'. I appeared on the programme together with a humanist, to discuss the question, 'Does God exist?' The gentleman who was producing the film had produced films from India about caste systems and untouchability, and I was asked to see the films and to comment on them. I declined, but in spite of my objections the interviewer continued to ask me about the caste system, and ironically he kept asking the humanist which god he believed in. Eventually I made a very attacking remark that within the limits of ten minutes I was mostly being asked about the rigidity of the caste system, whereas I thought I would be discussing the existence of God, and eventually the director was clever enough to sense my feelings and only part of the film was shown, where there was a temple scene, and then I was asked about the Hindu beliefs in God. During the 1960s, whenever I was asked to give a talk on Hinduism, inevitably the discussion came round to untouchability, the caste system, cow worship, and the status of women. Now, the questions are about the Vedanta, yoga and meditation. In most schools now comparative religion is taught as part of the normal school curriculum, and many British students have sought my help in preparing papers on Hinduism, and my colleagues have the same kind of experience.

I would leave the final comment on the situation to Mr. Bill Kitney, principal of the Mary Ward Centre for Adult Education, where I teach Sanskrit and Indian Culture. He says of my class: 'A great experiment in community relations is going on in this class. People just do not meet as strangers, they meet with a purpose. If sensible people can meet sensibly and take the initiative in breaking the ice and understanding each other, then this world will become a better place to live in.' I think we can achieve this if we approach each other with sympathy and understanding, without any sense of superiority of our culture, literature, and achievements.

13

The Meaning and Message of Islam

M. M. AHSAN

Islām IS AN ARABIC WORD SIGNIFYING OBEDIENCE, submission and peace. 'Islam' means to commit oneself totally to God. Submission in Islam is not passive but is rather a positive act of commitment to God, bringing attitudes and behaviour into harmony with the Divine Will. In short, a Muslim is one who follows God's commands and does not disobey Him either in word or in deed.

Allāh is the Arabic word for God and Muslims all over the world prefer to use this term instead of its vernacular equivalents. God's relationship with man is that of Master to servant, Creator to created and Ruler to ruled. Muslims look to God as the only source of knowledge and guidance. God made His Will known to His people through sending a Messenger with guidance so that everybody could earn God's pleasure and approval and live in peace and happiness.

1 The Five Pillars of Islam

Islam is built on two solid foundations: *belief* and *action*. Belief without action is of no use and action without belief is of no value. Both go together, they are, as it were, like two sides of the same coin. Belief in One God and His messenger Muhammad constitutes the first pillar of Islam. It is followed by four others involving practical obligations: prayer, fasting, welfare-due and pilgrimage.

(i) *God is One and Muhammad is His Messenger (Shahāda)*
a) *The Oneness of God*   God is One and Unique (in Arabic

140

tawḥid, meaning uncompromising and pure monotheism, the absolute Oneness of God). God is All Powerful, Ruler and Master of all. He does not require any partnership nor does He have any son or family.

b) *The Prophethood* God communicates to man through the prophets, demonstrating the way of life he should follow. The first man, Adam, was the first prophet. The necessity of sending prophets at different times was to bring human beings back to the right path of God when deviation occurred. All the prophets – whether Abraham, Moses, Solomon, David, Jacob, Isaac, John or Jesus (peace be upon all of them) – were chosen by God and were given the message that God is one and that His commands alone are to be obeyed by mankind. All of these prophets were Muslims since all of them followed the right path and were true servants of God. The office of prophethood came to an end when the last prophet, Muhammad (peace be upon him), completed his mission and was made by God to be the seal of all prophets. Through him the religion of Islam as a way of life was completed.

Some of the great prophets were granted scriptures from God which contained detailed information about the course of action mankind should follow in order to please God and to achieve salvation. Like the Torah, revealed to the prophet Moses and the Gospel, given to the prophet Jesus, the Qur'ān (or the 'Noble Reading') is also a book of God, the contents of which were revealed to the prophet Muhammad through the celebrated angel, Gabriel. The Qur'ān, being the last scripture from God, enshrines all the basic teachings of the Old and New Testaments and thus protects the earlier scriptures, the original text of which has been lost. Moreover, like the Old and New Testaments, the Qur'ān is the word of God, and it is therefore the first and fundamental source of guidance which Muslims all over the world follow. It is through the Qur'ān that we know that Jesus was not the son of God but rather a chosen prophet of God, born of the Virgin Mary. The Qur'ān is the bedrock of Muslim life and culture, uniting all Muslims, giving them a distinct identity and fashioning their history. It deals with all important areas of the human situation, such as the God-man relationship, political and moral principles, social justice, law, trade and commerce.

The second fundamental source of guidance is the sayings and actions of the prophet Muhammad known as the *Ḥadīth* (or 'Traditions'). Over the years, these Traditions have been remarkably preserved down to the minutest of details.

c) *Life after death*   This life is meaningless if it is not to be followed by another, where reward and punishment will be meted out to individuals according to their desert. Muslims therefore believe in an after-life and a Day of Judgment when all, individually, will be called to account for their conduct. Those who have led good lives will be sent to Paradise while those who did not follow God's commandments will be punished in Hell.

(ii) *Prayer (ṣalāt)*

Although all of a Muslim's life is a life of prayer and worship, he is specifically asked to pray five times a day: at dawn, just after noon, in the late afternoon, after sunset, and late in the evening when the last glow has left the sky. Men are requested to pray in congregation at the mosque. If there is no mosque in the vicinity, however, they may pray at home, at their place of work or in any place kept clean and tidy. Women are encouraged to pray at home and not to go to unnecessary trouble to attend the mosque. Islam has no priesthood, hence any Muslim, well-versed in Islamic teaching, may lead the prayers. The five daily prayers make a Muslim remember God constantly, protect him from evil and misconduct and induce in him high moral and physical discipline. Prayer in congregation inculcates a sense of community and responsibility, while providing at the same time a demonstration of disciplined thought and action. At prayer, Muslims face towards the *kaba* in Mecca.

(iii) *Fasting (ṣawm)*

During the lunar month of Ramadān, from dawn to sunset each day, every male and female past the age of puberty must abstain from food, drink and sexual intercourse. Logically, the demand to abstain extends to all sorts of evil: 'See no evil, say no evil, hear no evil, think no evil, and do no evil'. It thus produces a sound conscience, strong morality and civic sense. It teaches people to be kind to the poor and needy, and to experience and share willingly their sufferings. Annually, the lunar month moves ten or eleven days ahead in the solar year with the result that Islam has never become involved in fertility cults or other seasonal pagan activities.

(iv) *The welfare-due (zakāt)*
Wealth is a trust from God, hence every wealthy Muslim is obliged to share his wealth with the needy so that a balanced economic society can be achieved. This transfer of wealth is known as *zakāt* and is an obligatory annual financial contribution to individuals or to the Islamic state of at least 2½% of a person's annual savings, goods or merchandise. It is spent in raising the standards of poorer members of the community. It is given, however, out of a sense of *duty* and not in charity. Charity is additional.

(v) *Pilgrimage (ḥajj)*
Pilgrimage is enjoined only on those adults who are financially well-off and physically fit to travel to Mecca, a city blessed by the *kaba*, the house of God originally built by the prophet Abraham about three thousand years ago. Pilgrimage is obligatory once in a life time, although believers cherish a visit and return as often as possible. Muslims from all over the world, drawn from many different nations, of varied ethnic origin, colour and language, gather together in a spirit of worship and dedication to God and perform special religious rites over a number of days. The international assembly of Muslim people at the time of pilgrimage demonstrates Muslim unity, brotherhood and equality at its best. Every pilgrim, whether he be a President or an ordinary man from the street, wears the same unsewn clothing and performs the same religious rites standing and bowing, shoulder to shoulder with his brother.

2 The Islamic Way of Life

A Muslim's life is led in complete and total obedience to the commandments of God. Islam is more comprehensive than many religions, providing a complete code of behaviour for

living, from the cradle to the grave. It provides guidance in all
social, economic, political, moral and spiritual aspects of life.
The purpose of human life on earth, man's duties towards his
fellow men and to his Creator and Sustainer are all clearly
mentioned in the Qurān. And the injunctions of the Qurān
were made understandable by the prophet Muhammad (peace
be upon him) by his practising them. Through the prescribed
forms of worship man may attain moral and spiritual discipline
of a high order, enabling him to accept all challenges, to face
any crisis and to endure various trials and tribulations.

3 The Festivals and Festal Occasions of Islam

Islam has two major festivals a year, known as *'Id al-Fitr*, at
the end of the fasting month, and *'Id al-Adhā*, during the
pilgrimage, respectively. *'Id al-Fitr* marks the end of the fast
and on that day it is customary for the community to offer
special congregational prayer and for its members to visit
friends and relatives in order to celebrate the joyous occasion
together. *'Id al-Adhā* commemorates the sacrifice of Ishmael
by his father Abraham and on this day Muslims throughout
the world, in addition to congregational prayers, make a
sacrifice to Allah in the form of an animal, and share its meat
with relatives, friends and the poor and needy.

Islam has other festal occasions such as the birth of a child,
circumcision and marriage.

Children are considered a gift from Allah and on the birth of
a child Muslims express their thanks by giving gifts to the poor
and arranging an *'Aqīqa* party to which friends and relatives
are invited and which an animal is sacrificed.

Marriage is both the basis for social life and the beginning of
family life. Islam considers marriage to be a very sacred act
and a step towards a better, purer and happier life. Marriage
ceremonies are arranged by a couple's parents and the guests
consist of relatives on both sides as well as friends and neighbours. Extra-marital sex is forbidden and the penalty for
offenders severe indeed. Indeed, in exceptional cases, Islam
prefers polygamy to promiscuity and prostitution. There is no
sex discrimination: husband and wife are equal partners and

play equal, though not similar, roles in the shaping of both family and society.

4 Food and Drink

Islam regards only wholesome and good things to be lawful. Therefore, all kinds of intoxicants, flesh of dead animals, blood, swine and animals slaughtered in any name other than Allah's are totally prohibited (*harām*).

5 Islam in the Modern World

Europe has a population of between twenty-five and thirty million Muslims in a world community of about eight hundred million. There is a significant Muslim presence in almost every European country, communist and non-communist alike. The Muslim population of the United Kingdom is estimated to be in the region of one million.

Over the past fourteen hundred years Islam has proved to be an enduring religion. In the West, although its message at times has been obscured by wilful misunderstanding, it has survived any and every vicissitude. In the past, Muslims have made a significant contribution in every field of human endeavour. In the present context of world crisis, Islam can point to an alternative way forward towards the development of the human personality and the organization of society. Neither materialism nor communism nor any other man-made religion or cult offers peace and happiness but rather faith in God and the keeping of His commandments.

For Further Reading
M. M. Ahsan   *Islam: Faith and Practice* (Leicester 1977)
Khurshid Ahmad (ed)   *Islam: Its Meaning and Message* (London 1976)
A. Guillaume   *Islam* (Harmondsworth, Penguin 1954)
Abul A'la Mawdudi   *Towards Understanding Islam* (Islamic Foundation, Nairobi 1976)
Seyyed Hossein Nasr   *Ideals and Realities of Islam* (London, Allen & Unwin 1966)
Fazlur Rahman   *Islam* (London, Weidenfeld & Nicolson 1966)
Maxime Rodinson   *Mohammed* (Harmondsworth, Penguin 1973)

Joseph Schacht & C. E. Bosworth (eds) *The Legacy of Islam*
(Oxford, Clarendon, 2nd ed. 1974)
Frithjuof Schuon *Understanding Islam* (London, Allen & Unwin
1963)
The *Qur'ān* is available in numerous English translations.

14

Jewish Practice – Meaning and Relevance

PAUL SHAW

"It is related that an ass-driver came to Rabbi Akiba and said to him, 'Rabbi, teach me the whole Torah (Jewish religious teaching) all at once.' He replied, 'My son, Moses our teacher stayed on the Mount forty days and forty nights before he learned it, and you want me to teach you the whole of it at once! Still, my son, this is the basic principle of the Torah: What is hateful to yourself, do not do to your fellow-man. ...'" (Talmud)

Introduction

Broadly speaking, religious Judaism, in its diversity of forms, has gained in strength during the last decade or so. Any description of contemporary Jewish life at personal or communal level must begin with an account of the destruction of the Jewish communities on the Continent by the Nazis; the physical and spiritual traumas, and the subsequent painful and slow reconstitution of Jewish life and religious institutions in new centres, particularly the fledgling Jewish national home, Israel. The Holocaust constitutes a gigantic chronological backdrop to all our lives and a great deal of our thinking. Much spiritual and physical energy will still be needed to heal that jagged wound.

Yet Judaism remains a vibrant force in the lives of millions of Jews. (The world Jewish population is currently estimated at approximately 13m., of whom about 400,000 live in Britain.) For the religious Jew, every aspect of his or her activity is wholly penetrated by acknowledgement of the Divine presence in their lives. Jewish observance is very physical and even

147

sensual; a complete dedication of behaviour to the will of God. A helpful analogy might be to that of a member of Christian religious orders; monks or nuns, who by deliberately ordering their lives, their timetables, even their clothes, acknowledge by this change of daily routine the power of the Divine which they feel in their lives. (But with the important difference that Judaism is a way of encountering the world, rather than withdrawing from it.)

However, Judaism is a diverse religion, it contains many different strands of interpretation and emphasis. Further, in the post-Emancipation world, the nature of Jewish identity is very widely interpreted. The Jews are a people and a civilisation, with national, religious and cultural identities. Although all of these have their roots in the Jewish religious tradition, not all Jews today would define their Jewish identity in religious terms. Conversely, religious Jews differ in the weight they allot in their thinking to other factors of Jewish life.

Traditionally, Judaism teaches that the Bible is the Word of God; and that within the Hebrew Bible and the teachings directly expounded from it, lies a range of duties, celebrations and commandments that God wishes the Jewish people to perform. Every religious act – every fulfilment of the intention of the 'Holy One, Blessed be He' (a common Jewish term for God) – is known as *Mitsva*; and some very intensive, mystical teachers of Judaism hold that the performance of *Mitsvot* (plural of *Mitsva*) actively contributes towards bringing the Messianic Age which Jews await.

The religious Jew who, for example, deliberately refrains from eating pork or ham (meat which is traditionally forbidden to Jews), does so because he makes something as basic as eating habits an instrument of his personal acknowledgement of the power of the command of God in his life. He feels that he is fulfilling an unbroken covenant between the religious soul of his people and their God. The very act of refraining is in itself a powerful and holy act, with deep mystic, potent spirituality – a transformation, in one interpretation, of the worldly, the purely physical, the everyday into an act of worship.

In one school of thought, this is exactly what Judaism is all about – transformations. The linking of the Heavens with the

Earth; the deliberate contrasting and meeting between the tools which man uses and the inner demands of the God which he believes to have put them there. Judaism does not distinguish between holy and secular, religion and ethics in everyday life; the world reflects the creation of God, and man's actions inevitably must be measured against what Jewish tradition teaches is His teaching. So all things are simply either Permitted or Forbidden; Fit for use (as e.g. food, or clothing) or Unfit. (This is a very un-Western view of the world; Judaism in many ways is, spiritually, more akin in thought-forms to Eastern religions.) In Judaism there is only one 'yardstick' for action – the *Torah*. How does any proposed action link in some way with the dynamic religious vocabulary of Judaism? Does it bring a spark of the Divine presence nearer to earth? Does it transform a mundane object, or activity, through a connection with the dynamic of *Torah*, into an instrument of Divine influence?

The patterns of behaviour, of *Mitsvot*, spring originally from the Biblical text. Judaism treats the Bible as infinite in meaning and message. 'There are seventy faces to the Torah', according to a Rabbinic saying. Just as we nowadays find many different levels of meaning in the words and language of a poem, so Jewish religious teachers throughout the ages have looked on the text of the Five Books of Moses as vibrant springs of religious inspiration. Since the Bible was the word of God, reasoned the Rabbis, every word and every letter must have a significance charged with mystery. So they set about 'investigatingg' the words, even the letters, the contradictions, the apparent mis-spellings – but all was charged with spirituality, and the 'acting-out' of hints in the Bible acquired a dynamic of its own, and became authentic expression of the encounter between man and God. The fulfilment of individual Biblical commands – the exploring by transformation into daily activity the limits of the suggestions of the Biblical texts – stabilised into widely accepted norms of customs clustered around individual rituals. In time (the first codification of post-Biblical law in A.D. 200 was the *Mishnah* – from a Hebrew term meaning 'to repeat') these were codified. They provided a basic 'vocabulary of worship' on which later Rabbis were to build.

149

The framework of Jewish observance, then, is a body of traditional acts and patterns of behaviour, regarded by Jews as a holy way of life, which governs the entire span of man's activity – both his social relationships (termed by Judaism as '*Mitsvot* between man and his neighbour') and his purely Divine observances – characterised as '*Mitsvot* between man and the presence of God'. This entire body of Jewish custom is known as the *Halachah* (from a Hebrew word meaning 'to walk' – hence *Halachah* is a 'Religious Way in Life'). It is the practical part of *Torah* – revelation transformed into daily conduct. The act is ultimately part of Revelation. Jewish tradition contends that the body of *Halachah* was revealed parallel to the *Pentateuch*, and thus has equal status to it – indeed, the two are interdependent.

Here is the word of God brought literally to life. But far from imprisoning the observant, it on the contrary opens out huge areas of sensual and physical appreciation of the presence of God, via all the senses and feelings that man has at his disposal. It is a liberation of religion from the abstract and intellectual into the whole person, and the *Halachah*, accepted as authoritative by the observant Jew, ensures that his senses and actions are constantly involved in a thoroughly integrated way, with encountering, acknowledging and celebrating the *Mitsvot* of the *Torah* of the Holy One, Blessed be He.

The Power of Observance – Physical and Metaphysical

I referred previously to the mystical idea that the performance of religious acts – *Mitsvot* – hastens Redemption. This concept was first enunciated by Isaac Luria, a sixteenth-century mystic from Safed in Upper Galilee. Briefly, he states that the radiance of God was contained in a series of primeval vessels of light. In the act of Creation, these vessels were shattered; and the resulting splinters and sparks were scattered throughout the Universe. Each time a *Mitsva* (a Biblical/Rabbinical commandment) is performed, one of these sparks is restored to its place; when the repair of the 'vessels' is completed, the world will be redeemed.

Thus, according to this idea, every religious act of the individual Jew, regardless of whether or not it has immediate 'relevance' or meaning on earth, is believed, through its cosmic influence, to have a tiny but real effect on the progress of the world towards Redemption.

Clearly, 'Mitsvot between man and his neighbour' also have an impact on human society. The *Halachah* enjoins a wide range of obvious and not-so-obvious social duties on Jews – from the saving of human life, visiting the sick, establishing systems of justice, ensuring that all men may live and work in dignity and freedom, providing diverse forms of charity, to caring about the physical environment, public health and public safety. These are all categorised by Judaism as religious acts; and the Jew who arranges for the local Borough Council to repair a dangerous paving-stone has not only performed a service to society, but has done a *Mitsva* – a service to his God and ultimately, the world.

This, at a very domestic level, is a Jewish ideology of bettering the world – the impact of the act in society is paralleled by its metaphysical impact which also is a step towards a higher, more spiritual perfection.

The other category of *Mitsvot* is 'between man and the presence of God'. Into this category come, for example, the Jewish dietary laws, prayer, phylacteries (Tefillin), and the observance of the Jewish festivals. With the overriding proviso that the saving of human life – even in the slightest case of doubt – takes precedence over all other *Mitsvot*, Judaism does not distinguish in importance between *Mitsvot*. In a sense, even the division into the two traditional categories is not in harmony with fundamental ideas, which regard Judaism and *Mitsvot* as an indivisible religious system.

These are observed because they are commanded; their effect may only be construed in metaphysical terms – yet Judaism maintains firmly that they are of the Divine, and religious Jews will continue to regard them as deeply potent and significant spiritual acts. It should be said that these *Mitsvot* are performed with considerable love and joy; contrary to popular belief (prejudice?) there is nothing 'arid' or 'legalistic' in their performance. Many Jewish thinkers have also noted the spirit of holiness and spirituality which these *Mitsvot* bring into daily life, and their elevating effect on the individual.

Equipping the Individual

The impact of Judaism on the life of the individual also prepares him, in a unique manner, for confronting and coping with a spectrum of emotional and social challenges.

Judaism is not a philosophical religion; it has no classified theology. Apart from very few basics (monotheism, the belief in Revelation, and the belief in Reward and Punishment) Judaism has no dogmas. Thus the reactions of Jewish thinkers to specific social and moral problems – whether at domestic or national scale – vary widely. To be sure, each problem raised – for example, heart transplants, – will receive a firm answer; but Judaism does not deal in generalities, and every instance is considered on its own merits for a ruling of *Halachah*.

But in the cycle of religious observances, Judaism places the individual in a wide range of roles which inevitably enable him to appreciate the sufferings, anxieties, and happinesses of others.

Nowhere is this clearer than in the celebration of Jewish festivals and fasts. On *Pesach* (Passover) each Jew is commanded to regard himself 'as though he himself came out of Egypt'. In a remarkably modern way, a religious role-play is enacted during the course of the festival, in which the individual must actually relive the experiences of his ancestors – a cycle leading from slavery to physical and spiritual redemption. He eats their food – 'the bread of affliction', re-enacts their struggles, and regards the Exodus as his (and his people's) own liberation, relived and renewed *for him* each year.

Similarly, on the fast of *Tisha B'Av* (the ninth day of the Jewish month of Av), which commemorates the destruction of the two Temples, the Book of Lamentations is read in the synagogue. The worshippers wear mourning clothes, and sit on low chairs or on the floor as expressions of grief. The grief is not only empathetic towards those who witnessed the destruction of Jerusalem – it is an intensely personal grief which the Jew is enjoined to feel; for the soul of Judaism is timeless
. . .

On the other hand, at other times of the Jewish year – the festival of *Purim* (the feast of Esther) and the festival of *Simhat*

Torah (Rejoicing of the Law-an annual festival marking the completion of the cycle of public readings from the Pentateuch) – joy, festivity, and even religious ecstasy are *enjoined*. On *Sukkot* (Tabernacles) observant Jewish families physically move into temporary shelters for a week to eat (and sometimes sleep). Homelessness, the nomadic existence, man facing the elements – cannot be appreciated unless one physically puts oneself into that position. And Jewish families do so, to this day, regularly for one week in every year.

In every case, Judaism *introduces* into the life of the Jew experiences of extremes of feelings and emotions. In personal life, his religion commands the Jew to be actively engaged in the entire cycle of life, – there are no human situations, from the moment of birth to the end of life, in which a Jew should not be involved as a matter of religious duty. Thus, for example, Jews do not employ undertakers; the rites and preparations for burial are carried out by members of the Jewish community as religious deeds.

Clearly, I have not described here a philosophy; but I have tried to indicate – in a very elementary way – how Judaism tries to anticipate the range of human motivations, experiences and emotions which we believe underlie the structure of society. From his understanding of people and situations thus gained from youngest years onwards, no human or social situation can be entirely foreign to the emotional experience of the observant Jew.

Conclusion

I have tried to describe, in a very personal way, what Jews believe to be the meaning of Jewish observance, and some of the ways in which Judaism helps the individual to deal with the world. Within the vast range of Jewish religious thinking and commentary, contemporary as well as historic, there are many discussions of the social order, different moral problems and political dilemmas, with suggestions for their resolution. The unique modes of Jewish thought have produced many striking suggestions. (Some examples may be found in the books listed below.) But here I have strictly limited myself to the individual – what is the religious significance of Judaism to him; how does it furnish him (or, of course, her) with the basic tools of understanding his fellow man.

For Further Reading
D. Daube   *Collaboration with Tyranny in Rabbinic Law* (O.U.P.)
D. Feldman   *Marital Relations, Abortion and Birth Control in Jewish Law* (Schocken p.b.)
Louis Jacobs   *What does Judaism say about . . .* ? (Keter)
Norman Lamm   *The Good Society: Jewish Ethics in Action* (Schocken p.b.)
Montefiore & Loewe   *A Rabbinic Anthology* (Schocken p.b.)
L. Roth   *Judaism, A Portrait* (Viking Press U.S.A.)
H. Wouk   *This is my God* (Collins)
Strassfeld et al   *The Jewish Catalogue* (Jewish Publ. Soc. of America)

15

The Meaning and Relevance of Sikhism Today

MANJEET KAUR

SIKHISM, FOUNDED BY GURU NANAK (1469–1539), IS A young religion compared to most of the other world faiths. Moreover, the ten Gurus lived during an age of radical change when both East and West were to be shaken out of centuries of traditional social customs and dogmatic religious ideas. Sikhism itself was radical at the beginning and it is therefore, the more readily adaptable to modern thought and conditions. Guru Nanak, acutely aware of the narrow and ritualised channels into which people, both Muslim and Hindu, had settled, introduced reforms, some of which even today, have not been totally accepted. The Ten Gurus eradicated the caste system among their followers, freeing them from all ideas of high and low caste, and of ritual impurity or superiority. They declared all people to be equal as brothers in the sight of God. Sikhs were free to marry anyone who was also a Sikh and to eat with any person of whatever creed or station in life. The Gurus supported the full and equal participation of women in all areas of life, giving them the same rights and responsibilities as men and treating them with the highest respect and consideration. Sikh women may take part in any religious ceremony, while the practices of purdah, infanticide of girls and the ritual immolation of widows were forbidden.

In their religion, the Sikh Gurus dispensed with all rituals and beliefs which diverted the believer from a direct path to God. Their way was supremely simple: believe in One God who is the Creator of all and who is everywhere present indwelling in the universe as well as being without time or limit. He is the essence of man's own being and by His grace, man may reach a mystical and joyful union with Him as the culmination of all his strivings on earth. Man must live an active life of service and love towards his fellow-beings while at the same time keeping his mind busy in contemplation and prayer:

> Thus are chosen the leaders of men,
> Thus honoured in God's estimation,
> For though they grace the courts of kings
> Their minds are wrapped in holy meditation.
> Their words are weighed with reason
> For they know that God's works are legion.
>
> (*Japji*, 16: Trans. Kushwant Singh)

The Gurus rejected the idea of an *avatar* or incarnation of God on earth who comes to save mankind in the hour of need. Man is enjoined to make every effort to save himself while the all-powerful, ever-present Lord God may stretch out a hand in aid directly and at any time. The Guru, whether in the form of some holy and enlightened person (such as the Ten Sikh Gurus), or whether it be the Guru Granth Sahib (the inspired writings of the Sikh Holy Book), or whether it be the archetypal Guru-concept of God himself (similar to the Christian Holy Spirit), is seen as the guide who shows the way to God but not as intermediary to bridge the gap between Himself and man. In fact, God experiences man's suffering through every ordinary human being and is yet at the same time, transcendent, beyond suffering and utterly joyful. This evident paradox can only be resolved in the mystical experiences enjoyed by the fully enlightened ones who are blessed with God's grace.

The social ideals of Sikhism, already described, are acknowledged in western society and officially by the United Nations as the rights and ideals of all mankind. In many parts of the world, however, the freedom and equality of women is still denied. Among some of the more orthodox Hindu and Muslim communities, for instance, men do not think women are sufficiently responsible and mature to be allowed to work or go about freely outside the protection of the home.

Although caste distinction has now been outlawed in India, great prejudices and inequalities still exist there. In other parts of the world there is still gross poverty and ignorance through lack of education. The Sikh Gurus encouraged education since it was necessary both for religious enlightenment and for earning an honest living in the world. The Sikhs were also obliged to help the poor, which they did partly through the institution of free kitchens attached to the Gurdwaras (Sikh Temples) and partly through encouraging mutual help and support among their followers. They were also to defend the oppressed and to give ten percent of their earnings to charitable causes. Since Sikhs are enjoined to work for a living and to respect all toil, however humble, hard or dirty, no Sikh ever remains for long either destitute or a beggar.

All religions today are going through a period of questioning or reappraisal. Many are making radical changes in the interpretation of their fundamental injunctions and scriptural references. What Sikhism has to offer the modern world in the way of beliefs and principles is universally and eternally applicable. It can be readily adapted to any kind of society and to any period of time. It did not lay down a set of religious rules and regulations for man's moral conduct, but it set out general principles of morality which can be applied according to every situation, in any society or time. ...

In a horrified reaction against the gross materialism of this highly industrialised wealth and pleasure-seeking age, many young people are trying to escape, some through drugs, some through communal living, some through adopting bizarre religions or through following charismatic Gurus, some, more sensibly, by a return to simple agricultural life. Sikhism adopts the method of facing life, with all its difficulties, striving for the conditional improvement of mankind within the context of existing society and seeking salvation and peace even amidst the turmoil and uncertainties of this imperfect and material world.

Those who support the great world religions are showing signs of a new awakening towards a better understanding of each other and a greater respect for each others' beliefs and practices. Guru Nanak never tried to impose his religion on others nor did he assert that it was in any way superior to the others. He said that each person should live up to the highest principles of his own religion, not by the letter of the law nor by performing assiduously the correct rituals, but by following the true spirit of charity, love and worship which is at the root of all religions. The Gurus, with one voice, proclaimed that all men worship the same God but that we give him different names and that we have different visions of him and we express our reverence in different forms. Thus, the Gurus were probably the first to proclaim the value of tolerance and understanding which is only now beginning to be accepted by the vanguard of religious thought in our modern age.

Among Sikhs, there is no question of division regarding the religious and moral principles taught by the Gurus. There is, however, some division of opinion as to whether some of the injunctions laid upon them by the tenth Guru, Gobind Singh, are still relevant outside their original historical context or in present day society. Thus, many have abandoned the uncut hair and beard and other symbols of the Khalsa† brotherhood, though they still call themselves Sikhs. Some of those who adhere strictly to the tenth Gurus commands assert that such people are not Sikhs. It remains to be seen whether these outward signs of a Sikh will survive as meaningful and relevant in tomorrow's world.

Sikhism, however, is very much alive and active. Within the last twenty years, it has been raised from total obscurity to its rightful place to be recognised as one of the world's major religions. The Sikhs, whose home was originally the Punjab, have now migrated to many other parts of the world. In doing so, they have not abandoned their religion or culture, but they have taken it with them, establishing gurdwaras and installing the Guru Granth Sahib in the midst of all their communities. Literature on Sikhism is now available in many languages and it is constantly increasing while there is a renewed and searching study of Sikh history and religion both in India and in British and American Universities.

It is impossible to say how many geniune western converts to Sikhism have been made as this has only recently begun on any scale at all. Moreover, Sikh religious organisation as yet leaves a lot to be desired by western standards, and each gurdwara management committee works independently of all others. There is no world leader or spokesman for the Sikh religion, as this would be against Sikh principles. The Tenth

Guru delegated his ministry to the Guru Granth Sahib as the spiritual guide of his people, and to any true members of the Khalsa as the living authority in any Sikh community. Thus no Sikh in any eminent estimation of the world, can be acclaimed as a leader of all Sikhs.

The Shiromani Gurdwara Prabhandak Committee (SGPC), Amritsar, is acknowledged to be the principal authoritative body to which matters of Sikh theology or practice are referred when any question needs to be resolved. Thus, when the custom of wearing the turban over the long hair for men was set against the need to wear safety helmets, its members gave an uncompromising ruling that only the turban should be worn. The SGPC also compiled and published a comprehensive book of rules for the conduct of Sikhs and their religious practices, called the *Sikh Rehat Maryada*‡. However the SGPC is largely rendered ineffective because it is dominated by parochial and political interests, while outside India, the Sikhs have no central bodies which effectively unite or organize the various communities in each country.

Despite these undoubted shortcomings in organization, the Sikh religion is still in a developing stage and providing that mankind survives the present world political and ecological crises, it seems likely that the Sikhs will have much to contribute to world religion in the future.

†The Khalsa is the association of Sikhs created by Guru Gobind Singh in 1699. Its members must take baptism and wear five symbols: uncut hair (Keshas); steel bangle (Kara); short dagger (Kirpan); comb (Kanga); a pair of special shorts (Kachcha).
‡See Bibliography

For Further Reading
Kushwant Singh *A History of the Sikhs* (Princeton University and Oxford 1963), *The Sikhs Today* (Longmans 1959), *Hymns of Guru Nanak* (Orient Longmans 1969)
Kushwant Singh and Others *The Sacred Writings of the Sikhs* (Allen & Unwin 1969), *Rehat Maryada, A Guide to the Sikh Way of Life* (Sikh Cultural Society 1971)
P. M. Wylam *A Brief Outline to the Sikh Faith* (Sikh Cultural Society), *An Introduction to Sikh Belief* (Sikh Cultural Society)